COUNTRY LIVING

PAINT
RECIPE
BOOK

Liz Wagstaff

Quadrille

*To my mother and Mark and to everyone else in both families
for their love and support*

Front cover: *Aged and painted wood and
terracotta pots (photo: Debbie Patterson)*
Back cover: *Verdigris finish on a plastic
fountain (photo: Linda Burgess)*
p. 1: *Chequer-board and gilt stencilled wall*
p. 2-3: *Deep yellow mock-plaster walls and
an aged lilac door*
p. 4: *Faux marble panelling and a sconce
painted to resemble lead*
p. 5: *Granite effect on a plastic pot*

The publisher takes no responsibility for any injury or loss arising from the procedures or
materials described in this book. Materials, tools, skills, and work areas vary greatly and
are the responsibility of the reader. Follow the manufacturers' instructions and take the
appropriate safety precautions.

Consultant Editor Gabi Tubbs

Publishing Director Anne Furniss

Art Director Mary Evans

Project Editor Mary Davies

Art Editor Patrick McLeavey

Studio Photography Patrick McLeavey

Assistant Designer Jo Brewer

Editor Linda Doeser

Picture Researcher Helen Fickling

Production Assistant Kate Walford

Published in association with the National Magazine Company Limited
Country Living is a trademark of the National Magazine Company Limited

First published in 1995 by Quadrille Publishing Limited
27–31 Charing Cross Road, London WC2H 0LS

This paperback edition first published in 2002

British Library Cataloguing-in-Publication Data
A catalogue record for this book is available from the British Library.

ISBN 1 903845 52 1
Printed and bound in Spain by Mondadori Printing

CONTENTS

INTRODUCTION

Paint has been used for centuries to decorate all kinds of homes and in that time a huge variety of finishes and effects have been employed beyond the flat coverage of a simply painted surface.

Many of what are now regarded as traditional paint effects have their origins in the great houses of the European aristocracy and were later adopted by the rising merchant classes who wanted to share in those splendours themselves. In the Middle Ages in Italy, for example, it was the fashion for merchants to commission artists to paint 'hangings' on their walls to simulate the opulence of fabrics they had seen abroad. And the skilled art of dragging was developed in eighteenth-century France by those with more taste than money who wished to enjoy for themselves the elegant look of silk-lined walls.

Transformation, illusion, or more frankly deception, was usually the guiding principle, whether the effect was one of rough stone, luxurious marbling or the opulence of gilding. As early as the fourteenth century, for example, the art of gilding – applying thin layers of gold to surfaces such as wood or plaster – became an immensely popular way of imitating the real gold decoration which only the richest could afford. Similarly, a trend for simulating marble began during the Renaissance in Italy and France, although in time marbling techniques became enormously sophisticated, with some painters developing fantastical colours instead of the realistic greys and pinks and yellows.

The opening of the silk route from China to Europe had a profound effect on the history of paint finishes too. Items decorated with inlaid shell were traded with Europe and by the sixteenth century Italian craftsmen had found a way to repeat the effect and were inlaying shell using pewter. The following two centuries saw French, Dutch and German craftsmen using the same methods to produce fine *objets d'art* and furniture. Inlaid tortoiseshell, in particular, was highly prized, but demand outstripped supply so a technique for simulation was developed, reaching the height of its popularity in the late seventeenth century.

The eighteenth century also saw the development of other stone finishes with the fashion for simulating the look of exterior stonework inside the home. At first, the finishes were used on large areas and architectural details. Later, they were scaled down for smaller rooms and less grand objects.

Left: A Tuscan idyll. The painted chest, the simple yellow chair and the pale green window frame and shutters have all aged naturally. But this is a look you can create within days once you have mastered a few simple ageing and distressing techniques. Careful colour mixing has also contributed to the effect.

Many of the wood finishes explored in this book also began their lives in the great houses of the past. Wood graining, for example, allowed people to enjoy the beauty and elegance of expensive woods without the cost, as the finishes were applied over cheaper timber. Ways were found to simulate lacquer too, itself a costly and rare finish.

Today great houses may have the best preserved examples of traditional paint finishes, but there are other good examples of wonderful effects in much simpler public buildings and in homes and apartment buildings all over the world because alongside the grand tradition there has always been the not-so-grand, vibrant legacy of folk and popular style – demonstrated in this collection of recipes by, for example, the cool blue-grey colour palette of the traditional Scandinavian interior, the dazzling blues, soft pinks and warm ochres that outface the Mediterranean sun and the sober tones of the Shaker interiors of the United States. These are styles and finishes firmly rooted in the often harsh climatic and economic and/or social realities of a particular region, perpetuated over centuries by people for whom the concept of style has often, for one good reason or another, been meaningless.

However, some of today's paint finishes have a more recent history and, like that of the traditional finishes, it is rooted in the desire to transform or simulate materials. These are the techniques used to produce theatrical scenery and properties. Stone blocking, for example, is often used to imitate castle walls, and I have used ageing techniques to

Below: In the 1920s and 1930s Charleston Farm House in East Sussex, where artists Vanessa Bell and Duncan Grant lived and worked, was open house to the rest of London's Bloomsbury Group. Together they created the house's unique style of interior decoration, which still influences designers today. Almost every surface in this little bedroom is a subject for paint.

transform cheap candlesticks into rococo masterpieces and a leather effect like the one described in this book to create a Gothic screen for a production of Puccini's *Gianni Schicchi*. With limited budgets and tight deadlines the techniques developed from scene painting tend to be economic, simple and quick-drying.

Many of the materials used in the past are still available and experts working on great old buildings and antique furniture undertake restoration work using the same equipment and techniques. However, for less elevated interiors modern substitutes can work well, and, as the results are quicker, materials are less toxic and many are available in a wider range of colours, they offer an attractive alternative. You could, for example – if you happen to have a ballroom – decorate it entirely in lapis lazuli at a fraction of the cost Catherine the Great of Russia incurred when she did just that at her palace in St Petersburg using the real thing.

Painting walls has often had greater significance than the simple imperatives of domestic decoration and display. From prehistory, when people daubed cave walls with scenes of the hunt, painting on walls has been used for ritual and symbol. In Japan the spirit of Tao was expressed in paint and in India the lives of Buddha were recorded in wonderful paintings. Pigments and paints were considered sacred gifts

Left: The mint-green tones of this bedroom in Provence have been applied using a mock-plaster effect similar to that on page 84. Almost pure powder pigments create the strong colour, and the simple, hand-painted border makes easy the transition from bold wall effect to plain ceiling.

Right: Beautiful sixteenth-century frescos grace the walls of the dining room of a villa in Perugia in Umbria. Note the elegant pleated-drape effect: this is a good example of a paint finish designed to simulate cloth.

from the earth, often being used in ceremonies and festivals on buildings, garments and on the human body.

Many ancient civilizations decorated the insides and outsides of their temples and state and public buildings with paint. The Parthenon in Athens was decorated in vivid blues and reds with gold and black detailing, now almost eroded away. But close your eyes and a picture very different from the clichéd austerity of classical columns and entablatures emerges. The Villa of Mysteries at Pompeii was painted with limeproof colours over wet plaster in a fresco technique whose beauty was preserved in volcanic ash for more than 1600 years.

Inspiration can be found anywhere from the medieval frescos of Italy to the functional designs of Germany's twentieth-century Bauhaus school. Art and pattern books are well worth trawling for ideas. It is also fun to read some of the old paint technique manuals, where you will discover how lucky you are not to have to use cheese glues or scraped sheepskin to make size.

Above: A loose glaze has been brushed onto the walls of this room with its wonderful ceramic wood burner. The pale grey-green tones are straight from the Scandinavian palette (see pp. 74 and 131).

Right: This German interior was a long way ahead of its time. Designed in 1750 by a farmer who inherited money, the decoration was executed in milk paints, which give it the flat colouring associated with Shaker interiors (see p. 134). No part of the house has been painted for over 180 years.

INTRODUCTION

Left: Skilfully executed, the aged paint on wood effect (see p. 128) has great charm. Here Scandinavian tones of grey-green on terracotta give the piece an authentic rusticity that complements the items it displays.

Historical references are also useful for choosing colours. Using elements from the works of the great artists, for example, is an interesting way to develop a truly individual look for your home. Maybe the blues of Giotto's frescos take your fancy or some of the rich, dark colours Holbein's wealthy merchants wore. The possibilities are endless.

Remember that the paint recipes in this book can do far more than change the colour of a room. We all now recognize how cool blues and warm reds can transform a room's mood but take that a stage further and clever use of colour can transport you to other countries and climates. What could be more Mediterranean than those sun-bleached cobalt blues? Paint finishes can also revive some favourite memory. For example, a look that reminds you of the sea on a summer morning might be achieved with the translucent glazes of colourwashing. Or using some of the ageing techniques described here you could re-create the crumbling stucco of an Italian palazzo.

I hope these recipes will also open up for you the possibilities of painting furniture and other objects with decorative finishes. Junk furniture can so easily take on a new personality, and new, utilitarian pieces that lack life and interest can be fun to age and distress. The latter may seem like madness at first but the right paint finish can lift a piece that might otherwise have been simply commonplace into something unusual and genuinely individual.

Right: This hall-
way, with its fine
array of antique
furniture, is the
ideal showcase
for a good exam-
ple of the stone
block effect (see
p. 94). This finish
is perfect for a
space that lacks
impact and you
can use it any-
where you want
to make a bold
first impression.

There really are no limits to what you can do. Above all, have fun with textures and ageing techniques and experiment with the wide range of finishes open to you. Eventually you will feel able to adapt the recipes for yourself. Mixing your own colours also adds another dimension for you can match almost anything from a dish of butter to a leaf picked up on a country walk. After all, if the results are not satisfactory, a surface can always be painted again with a different colour or a different finish. Remember, too, that with a little hard work almost any surface, how-ever poor, can be prepared for paint, though in exceptional cases this may mean you have to opt for an aged, distressed technique!

Paint effects are a wonderful way to express your character and that of your home and the people who live with you. With this book as your guide you have within reach a whole battery of tradi-tional and contemporary effects that enable you to undertake glorious projects in any number of different styles. So go wild with your sponges, spatter, stipple and rub down to your heart's content. When you rest from your labours, you will have created something that simply can't be found in a pot of plain emulsion paint.

Left: Gilding:
ancient and mod-
ern. The carved
screen is decorat-
ed with paint and
gilded detail, and
the mirror, with
its rich colouring
rubbed back in
places for an
aged effect (see
p. 180), looks
lovely below it.

PART ONE

GETTING STARTED

Everything you need to know about
materials, equipment, techniques and
preparing the surface before you begin,
plus a special section on choosing
and using the recipes

*The simple leafy candle sconce was given a lead finish
(see p. 164), while the uneven plaster wall was textured
with sand added to the base coat and finished with a two-
tone colourwash (see p. 52). The amphora is a wonderful
example of natural ageing on painted terracotta.*

MATERIALS

A well-stocked collection of materials is important. You will soon get to know the essential ingredients and replace them routinely. It is not always necessary to buy the most expensive brands but be aware that cheaper brands may not perform so well. Most of the recipes use materials easily found in local shops but, if necessary, going further afield for the correct ingredients is worth the effort (see p.188 for stockists).

PIGMENTS

Paint is coloured by pigment, available suspended in oils or resins or in the form of pure pigment. Many pigments are derived from precious stones and minerals – lapis lazuli is the main ingredient of ultramarine blue, and chalk and powdered marbles make up whites and greys. This is why they are often expensive. Buy high-quality colour if you can. Cheaper paints contain 'pigment extenders' which just add body and cause colour variation so you use more colour for the same effect.

SPIRIT DYES
Highly concentrated powder pigments, they should be used carefully as they are very strong. Mix with water to produce good wood stains. Fabric dyes offer an alternative form of concentrated powder colour and are also good for staining wood. The latter are often sold in tiny containers – an indication of just how strong they are.

ARTISTS' ACRYLIC COLOURS
These water-based paints are available in tubes of various sizes and in larger quantities in pots. The colours are concentrated and superb for mixing with water-based scumble and emulsions to colour paints and glazes.

ARTISTS' OIL COLOURS
Excellent for tinting oil-based glazes, varnishes and eggshell paints, these colours are also good for producing wood stains if mixed with wax; available in tubes and in larger quantities in cans. The names of artists' colours are internationally recognized so, for example, cadmium red is the same tone in acrylic or oils wherever you buy it.

COLOURS

TYPE	USES	MIX WITH	TINT WITH	THINNER / CLEANER	TOXICITY
Artists' acrylic colour	Water-based, fast-drying colour for use alone or to tint water-based paint and glaze. Available in tube form.	Emulsion paint, transparent acrylic scumble glaze and water	Other artists' acrylic colours	Water	Medium
Artists' oil colour	Oil-based, slow-drying colour, composed of pigment and linseed oil, for use primarily to tint oil-based paint and glaze. Also use to colour wax and oil-based polyurethane varnish. Available in tube form.	Eggshell or gloss paint, transparent oil-based scumble glaze and white spirit	Other artists' oil colours	White spirit	High
Fabric dye	Water-based powder colour for use in making wood stains. Good range of pale colours; some strong colours available.	Water		Water	Medium
Powder pigment	Finely ground pure pigment for use in mixing paints and to tint water- or oil-based paint and stain. Produces very strong colours. Also use to colour PVA and polyurethane varnish.	Eggshell paint, transparent oil-based scumble glaze and white spirit	Other powder pigments	Water	Medium to High*
Spirit dye	Spirit-based powder colour for use in making wood stains, when mixed with water. Good range of strong colours available.	Methylated spirits or water		Methylated spirits	High

*Some pigments are highly toxic. Always read the manufacturers' instructions carefully.

POWDER PIGMENTS
These may be used for tinting oil- and water-based glazes and varnishes and for making your own paints. Once the only option for colouring paint finishes, they are still considered the quality colour by some. They are available in a wide range of artists' colours.

PRIMERS & UNDERCOATS

Using the right primers and undercoats is essential to the success of any paint effect. They give you the correct base for painting. Once you have chosen your recipe and your surface, refer to the appropriate page in Preparing the surface (see pp. 42–7) to find out which you should use. That choice is determined by three things: the surface on which you plan to paint, its condition and the type of paint the recipe specifies. Recipes using water-based paints often require different primers and/or undercoats from recipes using oil-based materials: refer to pages 18–19 if you have any doubts about the paints you will be using.

Always allow the specified drying time or you may spoil the final result. Most high-street DIY retailers stock primers and undercoats but for a wider range go to a large DIY warehouse, where you can also often buy greater quantities at lower prices.

Red oxide primer and PVA are versatile materials also featuring in the recipes, for example for gilding or for staining plaster and wood.

PRIMERS

TYPE	USES	THINNER / CLEANER	TOXICITY	INTERIOR OR EXTERIOR USE
Acrylic primer undercoat	Seals any unpainted porous surface and patches broken areas on a painted surface before applying a finish. For use primarily before water-based paint.	Water	Medium	Interior .
All-purpose primer	See acrylic primer undercoat for function. This is the primer to use when in doubt about a surface or its condition. For use before water- and oil-based paint.	White spirit	High	Both
Metal primer	Provides a stable base for painting metal and prevents corrosion; the better option when using pale colours (see red oxide primer). For use before water- and oil-based paint.	White spirit	High	Both
PVA solution or bonding agent	General-purpose adhesive which can be mixed with water or emulsion to make a resilient primer and sealer on unpainted plaster and other porous surfaces. For use before water- and oil-based paint.	Water	Medium	Interior
Red oxide primer	Prevents metal corrosion; the better option when using dark colours (see metal primer). For use before water- and oil-based paint. Also a good base colour for gilding.	White spirit	High	Both
Stabilizing primer	Binds powdery or porous surfaces, for example, on plaster, wood or stone, before beginning to paint. For use before water- and oil-based paint.	White spirit	High	Both
Wood primer	Seals wood. Available in white, the better option under pale colours, and in pink, the better option under darker colours. For use before oil-based paint.	White spirit	High	Both

See also PVA and EVA (p. 23)

UNDERCOATS

TYPE	USES	MIX WITH	TINT WITH	THINNER / CLEANER	TOXICITY	INTERIOR OR EXTERIOR USE
Acrylic / synthetic gesso	For use before water- and oil-based paint. Provides a silky smooth and resilient ground for painting on plaster and wood. Rubbed back, creates a powdery, textured surface.	Emulsion paint		Water	Medium	Interior
Oil-based undercoat	For use before oil-based paint. Protects any surface, providing a good base for painting, and obliterates existing colour.	Transparent oil-based scumble glaze	Artists' oil colour	White spirit	High	Both
Water-based undercoat	For use before water-based paint. See oil-based undercoat for functions.	Transparent acrylic scumble glaze	Artists' acrylic colour	Water	Medium	Both

See also Acrylic primer undercoat (opposite)

WOOD PRIMER
The ideal foundation for oil-based paints on wood, wood primer is available in pink and white.

ACRYLIC GESSO
Available in a palette of colours, this provides a smooth base coat on plaster and wood. Natural gesso is the traditional perfect undercoat.

METAL PRIMER
This primer prevents corrosion under oil- and water-based finishes. Also available in grey or pink.

ALL-PURPOSE PRIMER
A good sealant for a variety of surfaces, including those in doubtful condition, this is a useful item for your store.

RED OXIDE PRIMER
The classic metal primer, it also gives a good base for gilding and bronzing effects.

STABILIZING PRIMER
A useful primer for less than perfect walls, this binds flaky and porous surfaces.

PAINTS FOR FINISHES

These paints will provide the medium or basic ingredient for most of your paint effects. Uncoloured emulsion, eggshell, gloss and masonry paints are usually specified, and to them you add the colours and other materials that make up the paints and glazes used in many of the recipes in Part Two. However, premixed colour paints are sometimes indicated, often when dark colours are required and colour-mixing from a white base would waste a lot of colour. The chart opposite tells you whether the paints you will be using are water based or oil based.

BLACKBOARD PAINT
This gives a tough, opaque surface for an iron finish.

EGGSHELL PAINT
For a smooth, mid-sheen finish: tint with oil colour.

GLOSS PAINT
Specialist flat gloss is the best. I prefer it to lacquer paint (see right): you can build up the effect faster.

LACQUER PAINT
Available in a limited range of colours, this is a high-gloss modern substitute for real lacquer (see p. 170).

EMULSION: VINYL MATT
For a flat, matt coat with a chalky look.

MASONRY PAINT
An opaque coat for exterior use: this one has a fine texture.

EMULSION: VINYL SILK
For a mid-sheen coat that can be worked for uneven effect. Matt and silk: tint with acrylic colour.

MILK PAINT
For strong, opaque colour in Shaker and colonial tones. Also called casein paint.

PAINTS FOR FINISHES

TYPE	USES	MIX WITH	TINT WITH	THINNER / CLEANER	TOXICITY	INTERIOR OR EXTERIOR USE
OIL BASED						
Blackboard paint	Provides an opaque black, resilient, abrasive surface for certain metal finishes.			Methylated spirits	High	Interior
Eggshell (low odour)	Provides a mid-sheen, smooth, non-porous coat of opaque colour on any surface.	Transparent oil-based scumble glaze	Artists' oil colour or powder pigment	White spirit	High	Interior
Gloss paint	Provides a shiny, durable, flat coat of opaque colour on wood.	Transparent oil-based scumble glaze	Artists' oil colour or universal stainers	White spirit	High	Exterior*
Lacquer paint	Provides an extremely high-gloss, flat coat of opaque colour for creating a Chinese lacquer effect on wood.		Artists' oil colour	White spirit	High	Interior
WATER BASED						
Emulsion paint	**Vinyl matt** Provides a uniformly even coat of opaque colour with no sheen on any surface. **Vinyl silk** Provides a mid-sheen, uniformly even coat of opaque colour on any surface.	Water and transparent acrylic scumble glaze	Artists' acrylic colour or powder pigment	Water. Methylated spirits will soften when dry or partially dry.	Medium	Interior
Masonry paint: smooth or textured	Provides a strong base coat of opaque colour for finishes on walls. An emulsion paint, mixed with sand or aggregate for texture.		Artists' acrylic colours	Water	Medium	Primarily exterior use*
OTHER TYPES						
Milk/casein paint	Provides a uniformly dense coat of opaque colour on any surface.	Milk powder or buttermilk	Powder pigment or gouache	Water	Medium to High	Interior

*Recipes give instructions on how to adapt the finishes for exterior use.

SOLVENTS & GLAZES

Most of the glaze recipes in Part Two include a scumble glaze and a solvent. Scumble glaze is a transparent medium which extends the working time of paint and gives it translucency. This is particularly helpful when using special brush/rag techniques or creating broken-colour effects. It is available in water-based (acrylic) and oil-based forms. Solvents also lengthen the working time; some are suitable for water-based materials, some for oil-based. Remember the right solvent for the job is also the right cleaner: that applies to your brushes *and* your mistakes.

SOLVENTS OR THINNERS

TYPE	USES	MIX WITH	TOXICITY
Water	Cleans and thins all water-based products. Also use to disperse water-based glazes for decorative effect.	Transparent acrylic scumble glaze and emulsion paint to create glazes or with acrylic varnish	Toxic when mixed
Methylated spirits	Cleans and thins many oil-based products. Also use to disperse water-based glazes for decorative effect.	Amber shellac or french enamel varnish	High
White spirit	Cleans and thins many oil-based products.	Transparent oil-based scumble glaze and eggshell paint to create glazes or with gloss paint and some varnishes	High

WATER-ON-OIL RESIST TECHNIQUE Solvents sometimes play an essential part in the finish. For the shagreen effect, water is sprayed onto the oil glaze and left to evaporate, leaving the distinctive circles.

DISTRESSING WITH METHYLATED SPIRITS For the limewashing effect solvent is rubbed into a dry coat of white vinyl matt emulsion to create an aged look.

DISPERSING THE GLAZE WITH METHYLATED SPIRITS Although normally used with oil-based products, methylated spirits can be used to weather a water-based glaze for the verdigris effect.

INCREASING TRANSLUCENCY
Colourwashing is a good example of the effects of scumble glaze (here the water-based form) on a glaze-mix. Parts of the base colour remain visible.

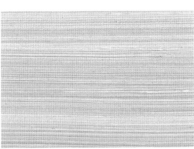

INCREASING THE WORKING TIME
Dragging requires long, continous brush strokes. Adding oil-based scumble to the glaze-mix gives you more time to work the paint before it dries.

GLAZES

TYPE	USES	MIX WITH	TINT WITH	THINNER / CLEANER	TOXICITY
Acrylic or water-based scumble glaze (transparent)	Makes paint appear translucent and lengthens the time it can be worked. Use with water-based paint and varnish.	Emulsion paint or acrylic varnish	Artists' acrylic colour, powder pigment or universal stainers	Water	Medium
Antiquing patina	Ages a variety of decorative paint finishes, in particular water-based crackle.		Artists' acrylic colour	Water	Medium
Linseed oil	An ingredient of oil-based scumble glaze (see below), but also used separately to thin or extend the working time of oil colour.	Artists' oil colour	Artists' oil colour	White spirit	High when mixed
Oil-based scumble glaze (transparent)	Makes paint appear translucent and lengthens the time it can be worked. Use with oil-based paint and varnish.	Eggshell or gloss paint, or dead flat or polyurethane varnish	Artists' oil colour, powder pigment or universal stainers	White spirit	High

ANTIQUING PATINA
Available in umbers and siennas for ageing water-based finishes on wood.

ACRYLIC SCUMBLE GLAZE *left*
Thinned with water and used in water-based finishes.

OIL-BASED SCUMBLE GLAZE
Thinned with white spirit and used in oil-based finishes.

WAXES, POWDERS & PASTES

Waxes, powders and pastes are important, versatile ingredients in many paint recipes. Mixed with oil colours, whiting or other ingredients, they are used to produce a variety of effects. Waxes also often form an essential part of the protective stage of paint finishes. Always check the chart for the appropriate solvents and thinners, as some pastes, in particular, can be difficult to remove from brushes and other equipment. Most of these materials can be obtained from DIY stores and artists' supplies shops. Store carefully and make sure all lids are secure.

WAXES

TYPE	USES	TINT WITH	THINNER / CLEANER	TOXICITY
Beeswax pellets	Mix with artists' oil colour to stain wood. Must be melted down before use.	Artists' oil colour, powder pigment and shoe polish	White spirit	High
Beeswax or furniture wax	Use for resist technique when ageing or distressing painted wood. Also polishes and seals wood.		White spirit	High
Black polish	Mix with silver metallic powder to create iron finish. Black shoe polish (but not shoe cream) is a good alternative.		White spirit	High
Clear wax	Mix with oil colour to create leather finish. Also polishes and seals wood.	Artists' oil colour, powder pigment and shoe polish	White spirit	High
Liming wax	Mix with whiting (see opposite) to age decorative finishes. Also polishes and seals wood.	As above	As above	High
White polish	Seals and polishes wood.	As above	As above	High
White wax	Seals and enhances wood.	As above	As above	High

BEESWAX PELLETS
Melt in a double boiler before mixing with artists' oil colour to stain wood.

BLACK POLISH
Use alone as a stain or mixed with metallic powders for an iron effect.

FURNITURE WAX
Use as beeswax pellets (above) or for a resist technique when ageing paint.

LIMING WAX *right*
Use alone for a limed effect on wood or mixed with whiting to age wall finishes.

CLEAR WAX *below*
Use mixed with oil colours for a leather effect or alone for enhancing wood.

WHITE WAX *below*
Use alone for a rich effect on wood or mixed with oil colour for a tinted polish.

WHITE POLISH *left*
Use to seal and reveal wood beneath light rubbed-back glazes. Also in liquid form.

POWDERS

TYPE	USES	MIX WITH	TINT WITH	TOXICITY
French chalk	See whiting.			
Sand	Gives texture and/or interest to decorative finishes, usually added to base coat and frequently rubbed back to add ageing. Available in various grades from fine to coarse, the latter usually used only with exterior paint.	Eggshell, emulsion or exterior paint	Artists' acrylic colour or powder pigment	Medium when mixed
Whiting or chalk powder	Combines with paint, PVA or liming wax (see opposite) to create aged, cloudy or dusty effects for decorative finishes.	Emulsion paint, PVA adhesive, liming wax or water	Powder pigment and, when mixed, artists' acrylic colour	Medium when mixed

USING LIMING WAX
Wax plays a vital part in the process of distressing the surface to create an impression of age for the simple fresco effect. After the glaze has been sanded, a layer is applied to retain the whiting, which is rubbed in to create a dusty look.

SAND
Sand of various grades can be used to give paints and glazes extra texture.

WHITING
Adds texture and interest to finishes.

USING WHITING
Here whiting was applied to areas of detail when the paint was almost dry to suggest the crusty, weathered look of aged lead.

PVA
Mixed with pigment, it stains or seals wall, metal, and wood finishes.

PASTES

TYPE	USES	MIX WITH	TINT WITH	THINNER / CLEANER	TOXICITY
PVA adhesive or white glue	Seals porous and flaky surfaces; used with water-based paints. Also use with powder pigment to stain plaster and wood.	Emulsion paint	Artists' acrylic colour or powder pigment	Water	Medium
EVA adhesive	The water-resistant version of PVA (see above).		As above	As above	Medium

VARNISHES & SEALANTS

These are often needed for the final stage of a finish so keep a variety in stock. However, besides simply sealing and protecting your effects against hard wear or weathering, they can play a part in the finishes themselves – either mixed with colour for decorative ageing or to provide an instant look of age (using water- and oil-based crackle varnishes). Most varnishes and sealants are highly toxic and must be handled with care and stored with the lids well secured. Always check the drying times and follow the instructions for applying additional coats.

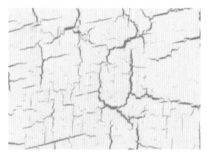

WATER-BASED CRACKLE
Used with water-based emulsion. The cracks are short and jagged. This is the varnish to choose for a stylized effect.

OIL-BASED CRACKLE
Used with oil-based eggshell paint. With wide-spaced cracks overlaying a network of hairline cracks, this is the varnish for an antique effect.

ACRYLIC VARNISH
Water-based itself, acrylic varnish is an ideal sealant for water-based finishes as it is quick drying and durable. Matt, satin or silk finishes are specified to enhance the effects.

CRACKLE VARNISH
Both water-based (top) and oil-based (bottom) crackle varnishes are used for aged effects on wood (see above). Follow the manufacturer's instructions carefully because the method can vary from make to make.

DEAD FLAT VARNISH
This produces a flat sheen for a tough sealant on oil-based finishes.

FRENCH ENAMEL VARNISH
A decorative sealant used for wood and ornamental finishes: available in a good range of colours.

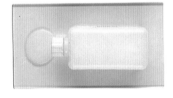

SHELLAC *left*
Available in several colours to seal gilded and bronzed surfaces.

POLYURETHANE VARNISH
Ideal over oil-based effects; primarily an exterior-quality sealant (shown tinted).

YACHT VARNISH
A tough exterior-quality varnish: for use over water- and oil-based finishes.

VARNISHES & SEALANTS

TYPE	USES	MIX WITH	TINT WITH	THINNER / CLEANER	TOXICITY	INTERIOR OR EXTERIOR USE
Acrylic varnish: clear matt, satin or silk	Seals and protects water-based paint finishes. Quick to dry and durable.		Artists' acrylic colour, powder pigment or universal stainers	Water	Medium	Interior
Crackle varnish	**Water based** Creates cracked-paint effect if applied between water-based base and top coats.			Water	Medium	Interior
	Oil based Creates wider spaced cracking if two coats applied over oil-based base coat.			Water (unusually)	High	Interior
Dead flat varnish	A traditional product, which seals and protects oil-based paint finishes.	Transparent oil-based scumble glaze	Artists' oil colour, powder pigment or universal stainers	White spirit	High	Interior
French enamel varnish	Seals and colours gilded surfaces. Also use to paint on glass. Available in a wide range of colours.		Spirit-based wood dye and stain	Methylated spirits	High	Interior
Oil fixative	Seals and polishes wood and distressed finishes.		Artists' oil colour or powder pigment	White spirit	High	Interior
Polyurethane varnish: clear gloss, satin or matt	Protects oil-based paint finishes. Slow-drying and durable. Also tint to age lacquer effect.	Transparent oil-based scumble glaze	Artists' oil colour	White spirit	High	Exterior
Shellac (amber)	Seals and ages gilded and bronzed surfaces. Also use to seal stencil card.		Artists' oil colour or powder pigment	White spirit	High	Interior
Yacht or exterior varnish: clear gloss or satin	Protects oil- and water-based paint finishes. Extremely tough and durable.	Transparent oil-based scumble glaze	Artists' oil colour	White spirit	High	Exterior

See also Clear wax (p. 22).

METALLIC FINISHES

Dutch metal leaf and metallic powders and paints, today's cheaper alternatives to real gold and precious metal leaf, have made gilding and its related finishes affordable possibilities. In many ways, these modern materials are some of the most rewarding to work with as they provide such stunning results. They are also available in many different colours and tones, giving you great scope for experiment. Take time to learn the techniques of distressing and ageing described in the recipes – they can transform sometimes harsh, tinny effects into opulence and beauty.

METALLIC POWDER AND WAX
Silver metallic powder mixed with black polish creates the darker and subtler of the iron effects.

SPATTERING WITH GOLD PAINT
Here the characteristic 'fool's gold' often seen in lapis lazuli is rendered with the least expensive form of gold finish.

JAPAN SIZE *below*
The traditional, oil-based size, it takes a long time to dry.

ITALIAN SIZE *above*
A modern form: fast-drying, water based.

SIZES

TYPE	USES	MIX WITH	TINT WITH	THINNER / CLEANER	TOXICITY
Italian size (water based)	Provides an adhesive, quick to dry base for metallic powders and leaf. Also use as a sealant on some decorative finishes.		Artists' acrylic colour	Water	Medium
Japan gold size (oil based)	Provides an adhesive, slow to dry base for bronze and metallic powders and real gold leaf.	Transparent oil-based scumble glaze to make size more visible or oil-based paint to give a good base colour.	Artists' oil colour and powder pigment	White spirit	High

PAINTS, POWDERS & LEAF

TYPE	USES	TINT WITH	THINNER / CLEANER	TOXICITY
Bronze powders	Mix with oil-based varnish or brush or blow onto oil- or water-based size to create a metallic finish on any surface. Available in tones of bronze, gold and copper. Cheaper than Dutch metal leaf and more effective than paint.	Amber shellac or french enamel varnish	Methylated spirits	High
Dutch metal leaf: copper, gold and aluminium	Lay down on oil- or water-based size to create a metallic finish on any surface; aluminium makes an effective silver finish. Cheaper than real gold leaf. Available in whole leaves or fragments (schlag).	As above		High when applied
Gold paint or paste	Creates a gold finish on any surface. Simpler to use and cheaper than gold Dutch metal leaf and bronze powders, but not so effective.	As above	Methylated spirits	High
Metallic powders (inc. graphite)	Mix with oil-based varnish or brush or blow onto oil- or water-based size to create a variety of coloured metallic finishes on any surface.	As above	Methylated spirits if mixed	High
Silver paint	Creates a silver finish on any surface. Simpler to use and cheaper than aluminium Dutch metal leaf, but not so effective.	As above	Methylated spirits	High

BRONZE POWDERS
Available in gold, silver, copper and bronze tones. Brush or blow onto size or mix with shellac.

DUTCH METAL LEAF
This composite leaf offers a cheaper but satisfactory alternative to real metal leaf. It is available in many gold tones, as well as aluminium (for a silver effect) and copper. Made in sheets 15cm (6in) square, it is also obtainable in broken form (schlag). The traditional gilding tools shown are a knife for cutting leaf and a burnisher with an agate set at its tip.

GOLD PAINT
Quick to apply, this is an oil-based alternative to gilding.

GOLD PASTE
Rub or paint onto a red oxide primer.

SILVER PAINT
Use as the base for an iron finish or as an alternative to leaf.

GRAPHITE POWDER
Add to paints and waxes to create a dark, metallic look.

METALLIC POWDERS
Available in a great range of colours, they can be blown or brushed onto partly dry size or mixed with wax (see p. 26) to create a variety of realistic and fantasy metal finishes.

BRUSHES

The key to perfect paint effects is using the correct equipment. Inferior or incorrect equipment will affect the result and ultimately make the job harder. There are cheaper alternatives to some brushes, but it is usually worth buying the proper ones, and if you look after them well (see p. 37) they will last for years. More DIY stores and paint supplies shops now sell specialist brushes and other equipment, and many specialist shops and manufacturers run good mail-order services (see p. 188). Always buy the right sized brush or tool for the job. Using equipment that is smaller or larger than needed frequently wastes time and may make it more difficult to achieve the effect you want.

1 HOUSEHOLD BRUSHES
Stiff-bristled standard brushes for oil-based undercoats, base coats and varnishes.

2 EMULSION BRUSHES
Designed with extra flexibility, they are used for water-based paints and glazes.

3 DUSTING BRUSH
Good for dusting down a surface after sanding, this also makes a successful, cheaper alternative to a badger softener or lily-bristle brush.

4 BLOCK BRUSH
This is good for painting roughly textured surfaces and also as a cheaper alternative to a stippling brush. First used to emulsion pebble-dash.

5 BADGER SOFTENER
Now usually made from hog hair, this is used for softening both water- and oil-based glazes on walls and wood. Available in various sizes.

7 LILY-BRISTLE BRUSH
A cheaper alternative to a badger softener but dusting brushes are cheaper still.

8 SMALL SOFTENER
See Badger softener: for more control on small areas.

9 GLIDER
A bristle brush for applying oil-based glazes and varnishes.

10 STIPPLERS
For taking off dots of glaze: expensive.

6 DRAGGER
Used for dragged finishes and for wood-graining techniques, this will create bold, uniform brush strokes on all glazes.

WOOD-GRAINING EQUIPMENT
The wood-graining recipes are created with painting techniques. But a variety of effects can be achieved with specialized tools. See also p. 111.

11 ROCKER
Made from tough rubber with an in-grained pattern, it is rolled over a surface to give a wood-grain effect.

12 FAN BRUSH
This is available in pure and imitation bristle. When pulled down over a glaze, it gives a fine wood-grain effect.

13 MOTTLERS
Used at the second stage of graining to create the arc effect typical of certain woods; interchangeable with the spalter. Various types simulate different woods.

14 PENCIL GRAINER
Available in various different sizes, this is used to simulate bird's-eye maple and mahogany graining.

15 COMB
Each side of this triangular rubber comb has different sized teeth. It is used for pine and oak graining, and for stylized patterns on a variety of surfaces.

29

BRUSHES

3 VARNISH BRUSHES
Traditionally used for oil-based varnishes, these flexible bristle brushes give a flat, even finish. However, they are expensive and, as varnish is difficult to remove, I prefer more basic household brushes for oil-based materials, reserving these for acrylic varnish.

4 LINING BRUSH
Made of pure bristle, it is used for painting accurate lines on surfaces. To ensure a continuous line, load the brush heavily with paint.

1 SPALTER
Used for smoothing oil-based glazes and the first stage of wood graining, it is interchangeable with the mottler. Various types of spalter are available.

2 LACQUER BRUSH
A pure bristle brush, available in many sizes, it can be used for applying lacquer coats and varnishes.

5 SWORDLINER
Designed for painting decorative thin lines on furniture, this is also used to create veining in marbling – simply twist the brush between your fingers for an erratic, broken line. It is available in many sizes and needs careful storage.

6 ARTISTS' BRUSHES
Pure or artificial bristle brushes with flat or round ends, these are available in many sizes. They are used for many decorative purposes, including freehand work with oil- and water-based paints.

7 STENCIL BRUSHES
These brushes have round bristles with stiff, short hairs that are designed to hold only small amounts of paint on their tips for working through cut designs. They are available in many sizes in pure or artificial bristle and are a cheaper alternative to stippling brushes (see p. 29).

8 OLD BRUSHES
Old, overworked brushes are useful for giving interest and texture to many finishes. They are also good for spatter effects and for dispersing glazes.

9 FITCHES
Hog-hair fitches are mainly used for oil work, but are also suitable for water-based products. They are employed for marbling, freehand painting and spatter work. Various shapes are available – round, filbert, long and herkomer – and the names describe the brush head or its tip.

OTHER EQUIPMENT

You need other equipment apart from brushes for the recipes described in this book. Most local DIY shops stock the items shown here and you may already have some of them in the kitchen or garage. Keep an eye open for large plastic food-containers that can be cleaned and used for mixing paints and glazes. Old spoons and other kitchen implements can also be utilized as tools for stirring. Always clean your tools and equipment thoroughly and allow them to dry completely before storing. The chart on page 20 tells you which solvent or thinner to use, and remember for water-based products warm soapy water is required. Store equipment carefully – out of the reach of children.

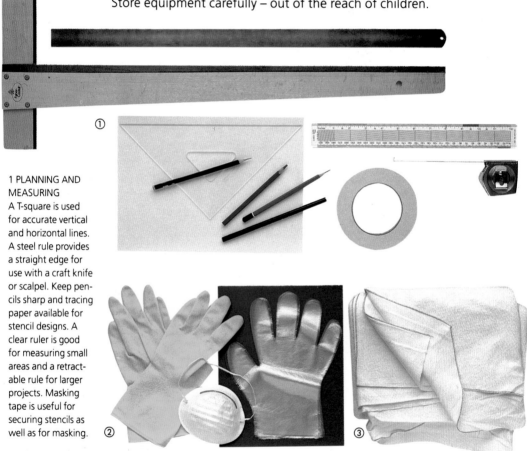

1 PLANNING AND MEASURING
A T-square is used for accurate vertical and horizontal lines. A steel rule provides a straight edge for use with a craft knife or scalpel. Keep pencils sharp and tracing paper available for stencil designs. A clear ruler is good for measuring small areas and a retractable rule for larger projects. Masking tape is useful for securing stencils as well as for masking.

2 PROTECTIVE GLOVES AND MASK
Disposable gloves protect your skin and keep you aware of the surface. Rubber gloves are for preparation. Use a mask with metallic powders.

5 STIFF-BRISTLED BRUSH
A good tool for cleaning painted and unpainted surfaces before painting.

3 DUSTSHEET
Plastic and fabric sheets for protecting floors and furniture from paint and dust are available in many sizes. You can use old sheets for the same purpose.

6 SCRAPER
Used to remove old paint, dirt and wallpaper, it will also remove paint from window panes.

4 WIRE BRUSH
This is used for scrubbing down painted surfaces and for removing crust and mould from metal.

7 STIRRERS
Old spoons, knives and pieces of wood are ideal for mixing paint and glaze.

8 PLASTIC PAINT KETTLE
Good for holding water-based paints and glazes.

9 METAL PAINT KETTLE
More adaptable: for holding water- and oil-based materials.

10 PLASTIC PAINT KETTLE WITH LID
Lidded containers are useful for storage.

11 JUGS
A jug measure and set of standard measuring spoons are essential equipment, so too are funnels for safe pouring. Foil dishes or roller trays are good for holding glazes when sponging and rag rolling.

12 BRADAWL
For 'woodworming'.

13 CRAFT KNIFE
For cutting stencils and distressing wood.

14 SCALPEL
This is ideal for cutting intricate stencils.

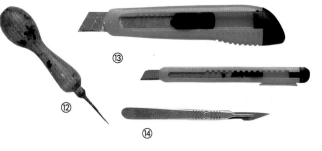

15 CLOTH AND RAG
Lint-free cloth (top): for applying wax and rubbing off. Rag: for rag rolling, mopping and cleaning.

16 SPONGES
Sea sponges are best. Tear synthetics for more natural effects.

17 ABRASIVES
Sandpaper, wet and dry paper and wire-wool create a 'key' for painted or distressed surfaces.

PAINT TECHNIQUES

In the recipes in Part Two you will find references to particular paint techniques. Mastering them is valuable because, once you are confident in your skills, you can begin to experiment and develop your own finishes. Many of these techniques can be adapted to the area or surface on which you are working, but, as a rule, it is sensible to use the correct equipment for each one (see pp. 28–33). To ensure success with the recipes in this book, follow the step-by-step instructions and refer to the additional advice given in this section as directed.

COVERING SURFACES

EVEN COVER
RANDOM COVER

Even cover
Working over an area approx 1m² (3ft²) at a time, apply regular horizontal brush strokes to cover. Repeat, using vertical strokes. Your aim is to cover the surface completely.

Random cover
Work more freely with diagonal strokes. Note the firmer hand position which allows more brush movement. The result: an uneven finish with some of the coat beneath visible.

SOFTENING BRUSH STROKES

BADGER SOFTENER
DRY BRUSH

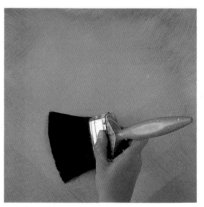

Using a badger softener
Hold the brush lightly by the handle so that you can flop the hairs backwards and forwards. Only the tips should skim the surface. Do not drag the glaze or eradicate the brush strokes.

Using a dry brush
Use a firm grip to flick the tips of the bristles quickly over the glaze. Useful wherever non-directional strokes are appropriate, this less subtle method eradicates brush marks totally.

STIPPLING

Stippling

The action is a light tapping of the tips of the bristles over the surface to lift off tiny flecks of paint and glaze. Stippling brushes are expensive and stencil brushes make an adequate substitute. The depth of the impression depends on the pressure you use.

An alternative to dry-brush softening, it also creates the type of even, non-directional surface which is valuable on panelling. This method of softening brush strokes has been elevated into a finish in its own right.

PAINT EFFECTS

SPONGING

Sponging off and on

For sponging off (right) you use a damp, clean sponge to remove glaze from a surface, whereas for sponging on (above) you sponge paint onto the surface. The techniques are otherwise identical. Compare the effects of different sized sponges and hand positions. Vary the shape of your sponge and the pressure on it too.

DRAGGING

Using a dragging brush

Note the grip: an index finger to steady the long, continuous stroke. Make sure the brush is tidy, remove any straggling bristles and hold the brush vertically as you begin.

Using wirewool

This is an easier technique because you are working closer to the surface. However, the effect is less pronounced as you remove more of the glaze. Use fine-grade wirewool.

PAINT TECHNIQUES

RAG ROLLING

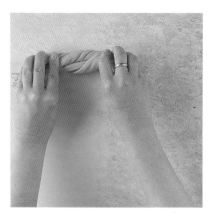

Rag rolling off and on

For rolling off (right) use a damp, clean rag to remove glaze from the surface, whereas for rolling on (above) the glaze is rolled onto the surface. The techniques are otherwise identical. Vary the tightness of the roll to vary the look: see the sharp-edged effect on the left. Note also the rolling action as it begins (above).

SPATTERING

Using a toothbrush

Flick back the bristles of the loaded brush with either hand. Fine, well-spaced spatter is created by standing about 13cm (5in) from the surface.

Using a fitch

For large, close-spaced dots stand 20–25cm (8–10in) from the surface or tap the ferrule (above) rather than the handle. See also left.

DRY BRUSHING

FLOGGING

Dry brushing

Note the grip: this gives you maximum control over the brush. Note also how little paint there is on the brush and the random brush strokes.

Flogging

Lightly tap the surface with a dragging brush to make small, vertical, random marks that help to break up harsh graining effects.

COMBING

Vertical combing
A steady hand and single continuous strokes are vital here – so is setting the comb straight at the start. Wipe it after each stroke.

Moiré
Drag the rubber comb horizontally across the wet glaze in continuous strokes. Then draw it from top to bottom in wavy lines.

SPALTERING
MOTTLING

Spaltering
The first stage in graining: brush spalter lightly down the glaze in continuous strokes. Less pressure is applied than in dragging (see p. 35).

Mottling
The second stage in graining: work from the centre of the grain, bringing the mottler up and over in arcs. Repeat, overlapping for uniformity.

CARING FOR BRUSHES

BRUSHES

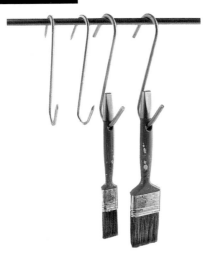

Cleaning brushes
For oil-based paint, pour enough white spirit or brush cleaner to cover the bristles into two containers. Wearing rubber gloves, dip the brush into one, stir it round, work off the paint with your fingers and squeeze. Rinse in the second container, scrubbing off any clogged paint with a wirebrush. Wash in soapy water, rinse well and squeeze. Rub the bristles between your palms inside a bucket and reshape while damp. For water-based paint, rinse under running water, wash in soapy water, and rinse, rub and reshape as before. Hang either type up to dry. They are best stored that way too.

USING THE RECIPES

This quick-reference section aims to answer many of the questions you are bound to ask as you begin looking at the recipes in Part Two. Read it carefully before you start work, study your chosen recipe carefully, planning your time schedule with care, and enjoy creating these beautiful and highly individual paint effects for your home.

CHOOSING A FINISH

Never rush your decision, especially when embarking on a large-scale job, such as painting a room or a big piece of furniture. Any paint effect is an investment of time, money and effort – and, unless you are very lucky, you will probably have to live with the consequences for some time. So relish the process. Make this book your bedside companion for a while. Then, as your ideas begin to crystallize, check the front runners against a few basic criteria.

- Can this finish be applied to the surface on which I want to use it? Check the colour codes at the head of the recipe and see p. 41.

- Is the condition of the surface appropriate? See the introduction to the recipe for any special requirements.

- Is the finish tough enough for the place I want to use it?

Now do a series of test runs on the remaining candidates. A 1m² (3ft²) sheet of scrap wood or card, primed as for a test board (see Testing opposite), will stand in for most surfaces. Study the results carefully under natural and artificial light, by day and by night, placing the boards in the room where the paint effect is to be used. The cost of a few tubes of paint is as nothing compared with an expensive mistake.

PLANNING

Once you have chosen your recipe, assemble all the equipment you need and enough paint and other materials for the job you plan to do – the coverage chart (see p. 40) will help you work out the correct quantities. Remember to check the appropriate preparation instructions too (see pp. 42–7) – you may need primer, undercoat and other materials as well.

Always take note of the drying times given in the recipes and plan your work schedule around them. Check the manufacturer's guidelines on each product too: drying times can vary. If the recipe is a long one with several different stages, make an early start. Any finish will look patchy and inconsistent if you have time to cover only half the area in a day. Never apply an oil-based paint late in the day if you hope to work on the surface the next day – the 24-hour drying time means that it will be nowhere near dry the following morning. Remember that drying also takes longer in wet weather.

MIXING

Follow the recipe instructions carefully for successful mixing with the minimum of wastage, and use an old spoon or stick, stirring well to avoid streaking.

The basic principle of the base coats for the basic recipes and the variations is simplicity itself. To your medium (water- or oil-based paint) add the appropriate colouring agents (acrylic colour or powder pigment for water-based paint, and oil colour or powder pigment for oil-based paint).

Glazes are by their nature more translucent and often need a longer working time so a premixed scumble glaze (either water- or oil-based) is added before the colouring agents, and a thinner (water for water-based paint, and white spirit for oil-based paint) after them. Always add the thinner last and slowly – it is easier and less wasteful to add more thinner than correct a runny mix with more paint or scumble glaze. Follow the same method for the variations.

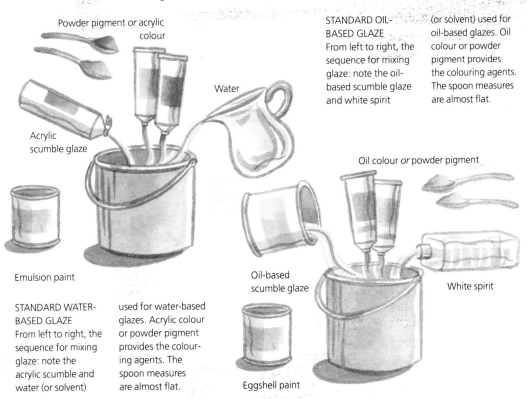

Powder pigment *or* acrylic colour

Water

Acrylic scumble glaze

Emulsion paint

STANDARD WATER-BASED GLAZE
From left to right, the sequence for mixing glaze: note the acrylic scumble and water (or solvent) used for water-based glazes. Acrylic colour or powder pigment provides the colouring agents. The spoon measures are almost flat.

STANDARD OIL-BASED GLAZE
From left to right, the sequence for mixing glaze: note the oil-based scumble glaze and white spirit (or solvent) used for oil-based glazes. Oil colour or powder pigment provides the colouring agents. The spoon measures are almost flat.

Oil colour *or* powder pigment

Oil-based scumble glaze

White spirit

Eggshell paint

TESTING

Always test for colour and consistency before applying paint or glaze to a surface. It is much easier to adjust a tone or mix at this early stage. Old pieces of wood or thick card make ideal test boards; keep some primed with white paint for the purpose. To test the effect of a glaze coat accurately you must apply a coat of the appropriate base colour and any previous glaze specified first. When testing wood stains or washes, try to test on wood of a similar tone or grain.

USING THE RECIPES

**MODIFYING /
CORRECTING**

Colour correction is simple if you follow the instructions on mixing. Add all colours slowly, checking the effect as you work, but take particular care with dark tones (maybe adding them last) and any pigment colours or you will waste a lot of white paint or colour adjusting to the tone you want. Try adding grey and umber rather than black or white: grey creates subtle shade, and umber softens colours that are too harsh or cold.

If a glaze does not move well when tested or lacks the characteristic translucent appearance, try gradually adding more of the appropriate scumble glaze.

Correcting mistakes of technique is always difficult. Oil-based paints and glazes dry slowly and can, with care, be wiped off with lint-free cloth soaked in white spirit. Remember to wear gloves and disturb as little of the surface as possible. With water-based paints and glazes you have to act quickly, wielding a water-soaked sponge or cloth, but you may have to paint another base coat and begin again.

COVERAGE

TYPE	AREA PER LITRE* in sq.m and sq.yd	TYPE	AREA PER LITRE* in sq.m and sq.yd
PRIMERS		**READY-MADE FINISHES**	
Acrylic primer undercoat	15m (18yd)	Eggshell paint	16m (19yd)
All-purpose primer	15m (18yd)	Emulsion paint (matt and silk)	9–15m (11–18yd)
Metal primer	10m (12yd)	Gloss paint	12–15m (14–18yd)
PVA solution or bonding agent	12–15m (14–18yd)	Lacquer paint	10–12m (12–14yd)
Red oxide primer	10–12m (12–14yd)	Masonry paint	3–6m (3–7yd)
Stabilizing primer	12–15m (14–18yd)	Milk/casein paint	10–12m (12–14yd)
Wood primer	12–15m (14–18yd)		
		*These are average coverages as provided by paint manufacturers. Actual coverage varies according to usage and to the surface on which it is applied. The addition of colouring agents, scumble glaze and thinner makes no significant difference.	
UNDERCOATS			
Acrylic/synthetic gesso	10–12m (12–14yd)		
Oil-based undercoat	10–12m (12–14yd)		
Water-based undercoat	15–18m (18–21yd)		

STORAGE

It is worth storing any paint you have left over: you may need it for minor retouching or for an accurate colour match if you want to repeat an effect. Oil-based paints have a short life, lasting no more than a month; keep them in screw-top jars or old tins with a tight-fitting lid – *never* in plastic containers. Water-based paints can be stored in plastic, but again make sure the lid fits well to avoid spillage and drying out. Label each container, giving contents, date and what it was used for. Add a safety warning on all oil-based paints. Finally, store all tins and jars upright.

SAFETY

- Always check the manufacturer's instructions.

- Handle all products and mixes with care – you risk inhaling, touching or swallowing toxic materials.

- Handle the following highly toxic colours with great respect, whether in powder, oil, or water-based (acrylic) form: ALIZARIN CRIMSON, COERULEUM BLUE, COBALT GREEN, COBALT VIOLET, IVORY BLACK, MARS BLACK, PRUSSIAN BLUE and ULTRAMARINE BLUE.

- Work in a well-ventilated area.

- Keep pets and young children away from the work area.

- Never eat, drink or smoke while working or store food or drink near the work area.

- Where possible, keep windows open while finishes are drying.

- Store all products and mixes away from children and pets.

- Oil-based glazes are inflammable – dispose of them carefully.

USING THE CROSS-REFERENCE KEY

Many of the recipes can be applied to a variety of surfaces. Every possible surface has been colour coded (see below), and colour tabs at the head of each recipe tell you which surfaces are suitable for any particular finish. For advice on how to prepare your chosen surface before beginning the recipe, just find the same colour in Preparing the surface (pp. 42–7).

For example, Colourwashing (see p. 52) can be applied to Walls, Wood, Plaster and Plastics; for advice on how to prepare those surfaces see pp. 42–3 and 46–7.

	WALLS	Suitable for brick and plaster walls. See p. 42.
	WOOD AND WOOD COMPOSITES	Suitable for wood, chipboard, MDF and plywood. See p. 43.
	STONE	Suitable for granite, marble, sandstone and slate. See p. 44.
	METAL	Suitable for all metals. See p. 45.
	PLASTER & OTHER POROUS SURFACES	Suitable for cement, concrete, plaster objects and terracotta. See p. 46.
	PLASTICS & RELAT-ED MATERIALS	Suitable for plastic, fibreglass and vinyl laminates. See p. 47.

WALLS

SURFACE	CLEANING	REPAIR	PRIMER*	UNDERCOAT*
BRICK				
Unpainted or painted: emulsion or gloss	Hose down with water. Brush with a stiff-bristled brush. Remove stains with a cleaner for kitchen surfaces. Painted: Rub down with medium- or coarse-grade sandpaper.	Replace pointing where necessary. Fill small holes in bricks with an all-purpose filler.	**Water based** Apply one coat of acrylic primer undercoat and allow to dry (2 hours). **Oil based** Apply one coat of all-purpose primer and allow to dry (16 hours).	**Water based** Not needed. **Oil based** Apply one coat of oil-based undercoat and allow to dry (16 hours).
PLASTER				
Unpainted: new or old	Rub down with a soft brush.	Fill holes with an all-purpose filler, and skim cracks with plaster. Paper with lining paper, laid horizontally, unless planning a distressed or textured finish.	**Water based** New plaster: Apply one coat of PVA solution *or* a bonding agent and allow to dry (1 hour). New and old plaster: Apply one coat of acrylic primer undercoat and allow to dry (2 hours). **Oil based** New plaster: Apply one coat of PVA solution *or* a bonding agent and allow to dry (1 hour). Old plaster: Apply one coat of all-purpose primer and allow to dry (16 hours).	**Water based** Not needed. **Oil based** Apply one coat of oil-based undercoat and allow to dry (16 hours).
Painted: emulsion or gloss	Wash with a solution of sugar soap *or* detergent and leave to dry.	See unpainted plaster.	**Water based** See unpainted plaster/old. **Oil based** See unpainted plaster/old. For unstable surfaces substitute one coat of stabilizing primer and allow to dry (16 hours).	**Water based** Not needed. **Oil based** See unpainted plaster.
Papered: sound or unsound	Sound: Wipe with a damp cloth. Unsound: Using a stiff-bristled brush and hot water, soak paper well. Remove with a scraper, working across the wall.	Sound: Stick down loose seams with wallpaper paste. For strong colours or metallic inks, apply knotting in solution (3 parts knotting/ 1 part methylated spirits). Unsound: Remove paper and follow unpainted plaster/new.	**Water based** See unpainted plaster/old. **Oil based** Unusual advice here: apply one coat of acrylic primer undercoat and allow to dry (2 hours).	**Water based** Not needed. **Oil based** See unpainted plaster.
Vinyl wall covering: unpainted or painted	Soak thoroughly and remove, using a wire brush and scraper. For obstinate areas hire an industrial steam stripper.	For remaining stages follow instructions for unpainted plaster/new.		

*Water-based primers and undercoats before water-based finishes; oil-based primers and undercoats before oil-based finishes.

WOOD AND WOOD COMPOSITES

SURFACE	CLEANING	REPAIR	PRIMER*	UNDERCOAT*
WOOD				
Unsealed: new or old	Rub over with a clean cloth. Sand with fine-grade sandpaper.	For painting: Apply knotting to prevent sap seepage and fill large holes with wood filler; then rub down with fine-grade sandpaper.	**Water based** For painting: Apply one coat of acrylic primer undercoat and allow to dry (2 hours). If not painting: Apply one coat of clear acrylic varnish *or* wax. **Oil based** Not needed.	**Water based** Not needed. **Oil based** Apply one coat of oil-based undercoat and allow to dry (16 hours).
Painted: emulsion or gloss	Wash with a solution of sugar soap *or* detergent and leave to dry. Gloss paint: Rub down with wet and dry paper and water.	Fill large holes with wood filler and rub down with fine-grade sandpaper. Renew putty in window frames wherever it is necessary.	**Water based** Apply acrylic primer undercoat to bare patches and allow to dry (2 hours). **Oil based** Apply one coat of wood primer to bare patches and allow to dry (6 hours).	**Water based** Apply one coat of acrylic primer undercoat and allow to dry (2 hours). **Oil based** See unsealed wood.
Sealed	Rub with medium-grade sandpaper.	Fill cracks with wood filler.	For remaining stages, follow instructions for varnished wood.	
Varnished	Brush well with a stiff-bristled brush. Take off flaky or rough varnish with a scraper; for obstinate areas use a gel *or* paste stripper.	See painted wood.	**Water based** See unsealed wood. **Oil based** Not needed.	**Water based** See painted wood. **Oil based** See unsealed wood.
CHIPBOARD	Rub down with a soft brush.	Fill large holes with all-purpose filler.	**Water & oil based** Apply one coat of stabilizing primer and allow to dry (16 hours).	**Water based** See painted wood. **Oil based** See unsealed wood.
MDF AND PLYWOOD	Rub down with a soft brush. Sand with fine-grade sandpaper.	MDF: See chipboard. PLYWOOD: See unsealed wood.	**Water based** Apply one coat of acrylic primer undercoat and allow to dry (2 hours). **Oil based** Apply one coat of wood primer and allow to dry (6 hours).	**Water based** Not needed. **Oil based** See unsealed wood.

*Water-based primers and undercoats before water-based finishes; oil-based primers and undercoats before oil-based finishes.

Note Some of the wood finishes – specifically Ageing, Staining, Rubbing off on Wood and Woodwashing – depend partly for their effect on revealing the grain of the wood itself. For them no undercoat or primer is needed.

PREPARING THE SURFACE

STONE

SURFACE	CLEANING	REPAIR	PRIMER*	UNDERCOAT*
GRANITE, MARBLE, SANDSTONE AND SLATE	Wash with a solution of sugar soap and leave to dry. Rub down well with a stiff-bristled brush. Found stone: Wipe with a weak solution of bleach to kill the spores of microscopic organisms and leave to dry.	Fill cracks and holes with an all-purpose filler.	**Water based** Apply one coat of stabilizing primer and allow to dry (16 hours), followed by one coat of acrylic primer undercoat and allow to dry (2 hours). **Oil based** Apply one coat of stabilizing primer and allow to dry (16 hours).	**Water based** Not needed. **Oil based** Apply one coat of oil-based under-coat and allow to dry (16 hours).

*Water-based primers and undercoats before water-based finishes; oil-based primers and undercoats before oil-based finishes.

Before stencilling and painting the motifs, these quarry tiles were sealed with PVA bonding. This was used rather than stabilizing primer so as not to alter their beautiful colouring.

A stone architectural detail is magically turned to bronze. It was first sealed with a PVA bonding agent and then given a coat of oil-based primer before black-board paint was applied. (Bronze powders, amber french enamel and satin polyurethane varnishes completed the finish.)

This Gothic head shows stone in its weathered state. There are lichens and mosses to clean off before priming.

METAL

SURFACE	CLEANING	PRIMER*	UNDERCOAT*
BARE	Remove any rust spots with wire-wool and wet and dry paper and water and leave to dry.	**Water & oil based** Apply one coat of rust inhibitor and allow to dry (1 hour), followed by one coat of red oxide primer and allow to dry (16 hours).	**Water based** Apply one coat of acrylic primer undercoat and allow to dry (2 hours). **Oil based** Apply one coat of oil-based undercoat and allow to dry (16 hours).
RUSTY	Remove light deposits with wire-wool or wet and dry paper and white spirit and leave to dry. For heavy rusting, rub down with a wire brush and then with wet and dry paper.	**Water & oil based** Apply one coat of rust inhibitor and allow to dry (1 hour), followed by one coat of metal primer *or* red oxide primer and allow to dry (12 or 16 hours).	**Water & oil based** See bare metal.
LACQUERED OR PAINTED	Sound: Wash with a solution of sugar soap *or* detergent and leave to dry. Unsound: Use a chemical stripper to remove the covering.	**Water & oil based** Apply one coat of metal primer and allow to dry (12 hours).	**Water & oil based** See bare metal.
PLASTIC-COATED	Sound: Wash with a solution of sugar soap *or* detergent and leave to dry. Rub down with wet and dry paper. Unsound: Carefully score the covering with a craft knife, taking care not to scratch the metal. Peel off and treat as for bare metal.	**Water & oil based** Apply one coat of all-purpose primer and allow to dry (16 hours).	**Water & oil based** See bare metal.

*Water-based primers and undercoats before water-based finishes; oil-based primers and undercoats before oil-based finishes.

Three stages: new (left), treated with rust inhibitor and metal primer (centre) and gilded (right). I used a blue metal primer designed for car paintwork, but red oxide would do just as well. See also page 182.

PLASTER AND OTHER POROUS SURFACES

SURFACE	CLEANING	REPAIR	PRIMER*	UNDERCOAT*
CEMENT AND CONCRETE	Hose down with water. Brush with a scrubbing brush. Remove stains with a household cleaner; a layer of sand will help remove oil stains.	Fill any major holes with cement.	**Water & oil based** Apply one coat of PVA or EVA** solution and allow to dry (2 hours), followed by one coat of stabilizing primer and allow to dry (16 hours).	**Water based** Apply one coat of acrylic primer undercoat and allow to dry (2 hours). **Oil based** Apply one coat of oil-based undercoat or for, cement only, masonry paint and allow to dry (16 or 24 hours).
PLASTER: large and small objects	Rub with a soft cloth.	Fill cracks with fine-grade all-purpose filler and rub down with fine-grade sandpaper.	**Water & oil based** See cement. Small objects only: Omit the coat of stabilizing primer.	**Water based** See cement. **Oil based** Apply one coat of oil-based undercoat and allow to dry (16 hours).
TERRACOTTA	Rub with a soft cloth and then with fine-grade sandpaper.	See plaster.	**Water based** Apply one coat of PVA or EVA** solution and allow to dry (2 hours), followed by one coat of acrylic primer undercoat and allow to dry (2 hours). **Oil based** Not needed.	**Water based** Not needed. **Oil based** See plaster.

*Water-based primers and undercoats before water-based finishes; oil-based primers and undercoats before oil-based finishes.

**EVA is the water-resistant version of PVA adhesive; use in conservatories and garden or utility rooms.

Identify the original finish and then clean. If the old finish was very glossy, sanding is important. Do not skimp this stage and apply several under-coats if covering a dark surface.

PLASTICS AND RELATED MATERIALS

SURFACE	CLEANING	REPAIR	PRIMER*	UNDERCOAT*
PLASTIC (soft and hard), FIBREGLASS AND VINYL	Wash with a solution of sugar soap *or* detergent. Rub down with wet and dry paper.	Fill cracks and holes with car-body filler.	**Water & oil based** Apply one coat of stabilizing primer and allow to dry (16 hours), followed by one coat of acrylic primer undercoat and allow to dry (2 hours).	**Water based** Not needed. **Oil based** Apply one coat of oil-based undercoat and allow to dry (16 hours).

*Water-based primers and undercoats before water-based finishes; oil-based primers and undercoats before oil-based finishes.

After the handle was removed from this old laminate door, the holes were filled with car-body filler. It was sanded smooth and primed before an iron finish was applied.

These plastic pots were sanded, given a coat of stabilizing primer and one of acrylic primer undercoat before being painted to look like granite (see p.152).

PART TWO

PAINT
RECIPES

Traditional and contemporary finishes
for walls, finishes to make all kinds of
surfaces look like wood, stone and
metal, plus ornamental finishes for
that decorative final touch

*A superb example of the water-based crackle effect
transforms a piece of wooden partitioning. Quicker and
easier to do than the traditional oil-based alternative
(see pp. 112–16), this demonstrates how a paint finish
can cheaply and completely change the look of a room.*

WALLS

Left: Terracotta blends beautifully with the wood of the painted cupboard and an intriguing assembly of antique and ethnic collectables. Fine sand was added to the base coat for extra texture, and it is this that has made the colourwash (see pp. 52 and 100) appear even deeper.

Below: Religious scenes and garlands decorate the walls of a Mexican courtyard. Bare stone, painted plaster and mellow tones are a potent source of inspiration.

Choosing the colour and finish for the walls is probably the most important decision you make when decorating a room. Remember the choice is a personal one. It should reflect the characters of those who live and work there and the atmosphere they want to create. However, daring to try something new is fun and may reveal a new side of you.

Undertaking your own finishes means that you can achieve an individual look in a way not open to you with premixed flat colour. You can design subtle colour schemes based on any favourite rug or painting. Or if you find inspiration on a trip abroad, many of the paint recipes here will help you reproduce the exterior or interior that has left such a lasting impression. The possibilities are endless.

Creating the right wall finish for a period interior was once time-consuming and expensive. Today successful substitutes have been found for the unusual and expensive products required and, using these recipes, you can easily reproduce interiors with an authentic look. Alternatively, and maybe more imaginatively, you can experiment with *faux* effects and modern broken-colour finishes to give age and character to a room in a way that flat paint just cannot. Any style of interior is now within your range – from a country kitchen to a baronial hallway.

Paint techniques can also be used to disguise some surface imperfections, which is much cheaper than having your walls replastered. A poor surface treated with the right paint technique can be transformed into a wall of character. Equally, a perfectly smooth, new wall can be given instant interest and texture.

Each room must be treated individually, even though you may want a cohesive scheme throughout your home. Remember some areas suffer extra wear and tear: certain finishes may not be practical for kitchens or bathrooms, and others need special protection.

Always consider scale when you are choosing a colour and finish. Unless you want an obviously out-of-scale effect, remember that paler colours give a sense of space and darker ones make a room seem smaller. This is helpful if you want to make a large room cosy or a small room more spacious.

If you are looking for subtlety, large areas of stippling or dragging are fine, but if drama is to be the keynote, these finishes will disappoint. Remember too that the colour of the base coat will greatly alter the glaze coat applied to it. The most striking colour effects are often achieved by using white as the base colour.

Many wall finishes can be used on other surfaces. Plaster mouldings and other architectural details, old furniture, plastics and laminates, for example, can be totally transformed using certain techniques. Study the colour codes at the beginning of each entry and check them against the cross-reference key on p. 41.

Above: Walls colourwashed (see p. 52) in soft earth and blue tones both re-state and diffuse the vibrant colours in the room. Note how the surfaces have been divided into a chequer-board of lighter and darker areas to add further interest.

Left: This ageing plaster was once colourwashed with strong sand and terracotta pigments (see p. 52). But eroded by time and neglect, this classical interior now appeals directly to the romantic imagination.

COLOURWASHING

Colourwashing is among the group of finishes that have their beginnings in fine art. Called the broken-colour techniques, they all involve distressing a semi-translucent paint or glaze over a contrasting, opaque base coat to produce subtle variations of colour. Specifically, colourwashing involves the application of thin washes of glaze in which the brush marks are left apparent to give the finish texture and depth. It provides an interesting alternative to flat colour and can be used to decorate period or modern, town or country interiors. Water-based products speed up the traditional process, which uses distemper.

A terracotta colourwash was used to decorate this farmhouse. Traditionally painted in flat, pale colours or simply in white, such interiors respond well to a rubbed-in wash technique. For this effect, brush the glaze on and then rub it into the wall with a cloth, using a random action.

BASIC RECIPE – YELLOW OCHRE ON STONE

INGREDIENTS

Base coat ▶ 1 litre white vinyl silk emulsion / 1tbsp neutral grey artists' acrylic colour / 2tbsp yellow ochre artists' acrylic colour / ½tbsp raw umber artists' acrylic colour

Glaze coat ▶ 500ml white vinyl matt emulsion / 500ml acrylic scumble glaze (transparent) / 3tbsp yellow ochre artists' acrylic colour / 2tsp vermilion red artists' acrylic colour / 1tsp raw sienna artists' acrylic colour / 400–500ml water

Optional protective coat ▶ 1 litre clear matt acrylic varnish (one coat)

EQUIPMENT

2 containers for mixing paint and glaze / 2 x 75mm (3in) emulsion brushes or 1 brush and 1 standard roller plus tray / large, well-worn, hard-bristled emulsion brush / badger softener or 1 x 75mm (3in) soft-bristled emulsion brush / 1 x 50mm (2in) varnish brush (optional)

INSTRUCTIONS
Base coat

1 Pour the vinyl silk emulsion into one of the containers. Add the neutral grey, yellow ochre and raw umber and stir well.
2 Apply evenly (see p. 34) to prepared surface with a 75mm (3in) emulsion brush (or roller). Allow to dry (2–3 hours).

1 YELLOW OCHRE ON STONE
The basic recipe described opposite: its subtle effect works well in traditional interiors.

2 BLUE ON WHITE
White vinyl silk emulsion is used for the base coat, and the glaze is coloured with 3tbsp cobalt blue and 2tbsp ultramarine acrylic colour.

3 TERRACOTTA ON STONE
The stone base follows the basic recipe, and the glaze is coloured with 3tbsp venetian red and 1tbsp yellow ochre. A large brush stroke was used.

4 LILAC ON WHITE
This bold, modern colourway works well in traditional rooms too. The base is white vinyl silk emulsion, and just 3tbsp brilliant purple colour the glaze coat.

5 MINK ON WHITE
A soft, neutral look for a period home or modern interior: white vinyl silk emulsion for the base, and 2tbsp neutral grey and 2tbsp bronze ochre to colour the glaze coat. Bold cross-hatching was used to create the diamond effect.

6 GREEN ON WHITE
The glaze is coloured with 3tbsp bright green over a base of white vinyl silk emulsion, and a bold random brush stroke was used.

COLOURWASHING

Glaze coat

1 Pour the vinyl matt emulsion into the other container. Add the acrylic scumble, yellow ochre, vermilion red, raw sienna, and water (a little at a time) and stir well until you have a runny but not too thin glaze. The right consistency is important here – the base coat should show through the glaze in the final effect.

2 Apply the glaze coat, using a 75mm (3in) emulsion brush. Work with random strokes (see p. 34), concentrating on an area of no more than 1m² (3ft²) at a time. If you want a more even effect, use arc-like brush strokes instead.

3 Using the dry hard-bristled brush, go quickly over the surface again, working with random strokes in all directions.

4 Holding the badger softener (or soft-bristled brush), skim the surface lightly, just touching it with the brush (see p. 34). This softens the brush strokes, but take care – overdo it and you will drag the glaze. Leave to dry (2 hours).

Notes You can repeat the glaze stage if you want a greater depth of colour. Emulsion paint and scumble glaze together dry to a tough finish but, if you are colourwashing an area that will receive a lot of wear, such as a hallway, it is best to protect it with one or two coats of varnish, allowing 2–3 hours for each coat to dry.

When colourwashing on wood, make sure you apply both base and glaze coats in the direction of the grain. Brush on the base coat and, when dry, rub on the glaze using a cloth. Soften the glaze coat as in step 4 above. Again, apply one or two coats of varnish if required.

Exterior use Substitute smooth masonry paint in the base coat and finish with two coats of matt polyurethane varnish.

Soft blue tones have been used to colourwash this hallway. An ideal use of a simple colour effect, it has brightened a narrow, slightly gloomy passageway, and the small amount of ochre used in the glaze mix has taken the coldness out of the end effect.

This simple MDF magazine rack has had an ochre colourwash applied over a stone base coat, following the ingredients given in the basic recipe. The freehand and stencilled decoration are in the Bloomsbury style (see p.184).

SPONGING OFF AND ON

Sponging is a modern broken-colour technique. Natural sponge, moistened with water or soaked in glaze, is used over a contrasting glaze or opaque base coat to produce a softly mottled effect – either by removing or adding colour. I like to combine the two methods in a versatile finish which produces both subtle and striking results: pastel tones create an airy lightness, while stronger, related colours give rich, deep tones. Use sea sponges if you can – they create more interesting textures than the uniform marks made by synthetic household sponges.

BASIC RECIPE – GREY ON STONE

INGREDIENTS

Base coat ▶ 1 litre white vinyl silk emulsion / 2tbsp burnt umber artists' acrylic colour / $^{1}/_{2}$tsp ultramarine artists' acrylic colour / $^{1}/_{2}$tbsp mars black artists' acrylic colour

First glaze coat ▶ 500ml white vinyl matt emulsion / 250ml acrylic scumble glaze (transparent) / 2tbsp neutral grey artists' acrylic colour / 1tbsp burnt umber artists' acrylic colour / $^{1}/_{4}$tbsp mars black artists' acrylic colour / 200ml water

Second glaze coat ▶ 500ml white vinyl matt emulsion / 250ml acrylic scumble glaze / 2tbsp mars black artists' acrylic colour / $^{1}/_{2}$tbsp burnt umber artists' acrylic colour / 250ml water

Optional protective coat ▶ 1 litre clear matt acrylic varnish (one coat)

EQUIPMENT

3 containers for mixing paint and glaze / 2 x 75mm (3in) emulsion brushes or 1 standard roller / roller tray / sea sponges in various sizes / water for dampening and rinsing sponges / disposable gloves / 1 x 50mm (2in) varnish brush (optional)

INSTRUCTIONS
Base coat

1 Pour the vinyl silk emulsion into one of the containers. Add the burnt umber, ultramarine and mars black and stir well.
2 Apply evenly (see p. 34) to prepared surface with a 75mm (3in) emulsion brush (or roller). Allow to dry (2–3 hours).

First glaze coat

1 Pour the vinyl matt emulsion into a second container. Add the acrylic scumble, neutral grey, burnt umber, mars black, and water (a little at a time) and stir well.
2 Apply an even coat of glaze using a 75mm (3in) emulsion brush and covering the base coat completely. (You can use a roller if you prefer, but only when applying the glaze to large areas.)
3 Immerse one of the sponges in water and wring out until almost dry. Put on the gloves and apply it to the surface, partially removing the glaze with soft dabbing movements (see p. 35). Vary your wrist position to create a variety of effects and strokes. You can also create varied effects with sponges of different sizes. Allow to dry (1–2 hours.)

Second glaze coat

1 Pour the vinyl matt emulsion into a third container. Add the acrylic scumble, mars black, burnt umber, and water (a little at a time – this glaze must be more watery than the first). Stir well.

2 Pour a little of the glaze into the clean roller tray, topping up as required. (Small quantities reduce the risk of overloading the sponge.)

3 Put on the gloves and, using another slightly damp sponge, apply the glaze to the wall in light dabbing movements, turning the sponge to vary the pattern. Again, sponges of varying size will help. Rinse them in water regularly to prevent them from clogging. Allow to dry (2 hours).

Notes Apply one or two coats of varnish for a hardwearing surface, allowing 2–3 hours for each coat to dry. The combination of these techniques gives greater depth to the colour and finish but you can use either of them alone if you wish.

❶ GREY ON STONE
The basic recipe: an ideal treatment for a traditional interior. Above the dado rail the grey glaze has simply been sponged off; below it the same glaze has been sponged off and then on.

❷ DUSKY PINK ON CORAL
The coral base coat is coloured with 2tbsp cadmium red and 1tbsp raw umber, and the glaze with 2tbsp cadmium red, 1tbsp raw umber and ¹/₂tbsp neutral grey. These rich tones work well in traditional or modern interiors.

❸ OCHRE ON SAND
A neutral look to complement natural fabrics: colour the base coat with 2tbsp yellow ochre and 1tbsp raw umber, and the glaze with 3tbsp yellow ochre.

RAG ROLLING OFF AND ON

Rag rolling is relatively quick and easy to undertake. The basic method is to distress a surface by using twisted lint-free cloth to remove and work the paint or glaze. Two or more colours can be used and a mixture of ragging off and on (that is, removing and then applying colour) gives an interesting effect, adding greatly to the depth of the finish. Rag rolling is an excellent way to cover poor surfaces, although good preparation is a must as the glaze tends to collect and darken in holes or cracks. It is wise to enlist a second pair of hands because the glaze dries quickly, and it is best not to overwork the surface as the effect will appear too patchy. Rag rolling is commonly used in subtle colour combinations to add instant age to a room because it simulates the appearance of old walls, but it can be adapted for a more modern look by the use of colour. A pale tone over a darker base can be attractive and unusual, and a bright glaze over a contrasting but equally bright base coat can give a stunning end result. The look can also be changed by using different materials to work the glaze. Plastic bags, lace, screwed-up paper and scraps of carpet can be effective, but take care to trim off any loose ends.

BASIC RECIPE – COBALT ON DUCK-EGG BLUE

INGREDIENTS

Base coat ▶ 1 litre white vinyl silk emulsion / 1tbsp cobalt blue artists' acrylic colour / 1/2tbsp cobalt green artists' acrylic colour / 1/2tbsp yellow oxide artists' acrylic colour

Glaze coats ▶ 500ml white vinyl matt emulsion / 500ml acrylic scumble glaze (transparent) / 2tbsp cobalt blue artists' acrylic colour / 2tsp cobalt green artists' acrylic colour / 500ml water

Optional protective coat ▶ 1 litre clear silk or matt acrylic varnish (one coat)

EQUIPMENT

3 containers for mixing paint and glaze / 2 x 75mm (3in) emulsion brushes or 1 standard roller / roller tray / lint-free cotton rags (45cm²/18in²) / water to dampen rags / disposable gloves / 1 x 50mm (2in) varnish brush (optional)

INSTRUCTIONS
Base coat

1 Pour the vinyl silk emulsion into one of the containers. Add the cobalt blue, cobalt green and yellow oxide and stir well.
2 Apply evenly (see p. 34) to prepared surface with a 75mm (3in) emulsion brush (or roller). Allow to dry (2–3 hours).

First glaze coat

1 Pour the vinyl matt emulsion into a second container. Add the acrylic scumble, cobalt blue, cobalt green, and water (a little at a time), and stir well. Set aside half the resulting glaze for the second glaze coat in a third container.
2 Apply the first batch of glaze to the surface with a 75mm (3in) emulsion brush (or roller) in horizontal and vertical strokes for an even finish, covering the base coat completely.
3 Immerse a rag in water and then wring it out until almost dry. Put on the gloves and wear for the remainder of this

❶ COBALT ON DUCK-EGG BLUE
The basic recipe: although the base coat is barely seen, the translucent nature of the cobalt glaze means that the softer base tone gives depth to the effect. The fineness and closeness of the finish are the result of rag rolling off and on.

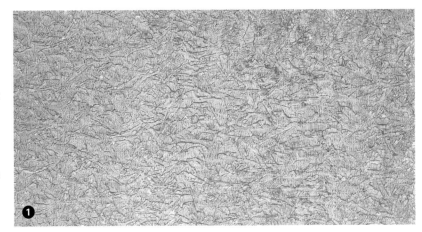

❷ OCHRE ON STONE
The base is coloured with 2tbsp bronze ochre and 1tbsp yellow ochre, the glaze with 3tbsp yellow ochre and ¹/₂tbsp raw sienna. Here ragging on is used for a typically Italian look.

❸ PINK ON OYSTER
A ragged-off glaze: 2tbsp burnt umber, 1tbsp raw sienna and ¹/₂tbsp yellow ochre colour the base, and 2tbsp cadmium red, 1tbsp titanium white and ¹/₂tbsp burnt umber the dusty pink.

④ TERRACOTTA ON SAND
A strong effect created by rag rolling off and on, this lends itself to traditional interiors: 2tbsp yellow ochre and 1¹/₂tbsp red oxide tint the base, while the glaze employs 2tbsp yellow ochre, 2tbsp red oxide and just ¹/₂tbsp raw umber.

⑤ AQUA ON GREEN
The base tone is coloured with 2tbsp viridian green and ¹/₂tbsp cobalt blue, while the deeper glaze uses 3tbsp viridian green, 1tbsp cobalt blue and 1tsp raw umber. Only ragging off is used.

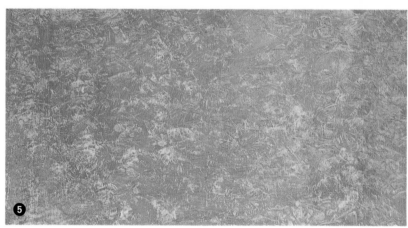

⑥ BLUEBERRY ON LILAC
The base coat is a premixed deep blueberry emulsion, and the lilac tone is created by mixing 2tbsp deep lilac and 1tbsp titanium white. Here the glaze is paler than the base coat for a striking modern effect.

stage. Roll the rag up, fold it in half and, holding both ends in one hand, twist into a sausage shape.

4 Holding the twisted rag firmly at either end, roll the rag over the glazed surface, working from top to bottom in a vertical strip as wide as the rag roll itself (see p. 36). Rinse and retwist the rag regularly to prevent clogging. Continue working from top to bottom in the same way, overlapping the strips by 1cm (¹/₂in) so the pattern is not too regular. Do not

rework areas or you will spoil the even finish. Leave to dry (2 hours).

Second glaze coat

1 Pour a little of the reserved glaze into the roller tray. (Small quantities reduce the risk of overloading the rag.)

2 Put on the gloves and then immerse a rag in the glaze and wring out. Roll and twist it into a sausage shape as described opposite.

3 Using the action as described in First glaze coat, step 4, roll glaze onto the first coat. Retwist the rag as required and recharge it with glaze whenever the finish becomes too light. Try to keep the effect as even as possible and avoid a stripy look by overlapping the strips by no more than 1cm (1/2in). Leave to dry (2 hours).

Notes Apply one or two coats of varnish for a hardwearing finish, allowing 2–3 hours for each coat to dry.

This friendly farmhouse kitchen has been rag rolled in soft ochre tones, an ideal finish for retaining the period, country feel of such a room. Its hardwearing qualities also make it an excellent choice. The simple, 'handstitched pelmet' border which joins wall and ceiling is an original, highly appropriate solution.

DRAGGING

Developed in the eighteenth century, dragging derives from the techniques of wood graining. Translucent glaze is brushed onto a base coat and a clean, long-haired brush is drawn from top to bottom to reveal the base colour in a series of fine lines. Traditionally a dark, oil-based glaze was used and oil-based paints remain the more satisfactory medium because they dry more slowly than water-based ones, allowing for longer working, and the intensity of oil colour gives a better result. Attempt it only on smooth surfaces – lumps and bumps spoil the vertical lines.

BASIC RECIPE – OIL-BASED DEEP BLUE ON WHITE

INGREDIENTS

Base coat ▶ 1 litre white low-odour eggshell paint
Glaze coat ▶ 500ml premixed oil-based scumble glaze (transparent) / 2tbsp ultramarine artists' oil colour / 1tbsp prussian blue artists' oil colour / $\frac{1}{2}$tsp yellow ochre artists' oil colour / 150ml white spirit
Protective coat ▶ 1 litre oil-based clear dead flat varnish

EQUIPMENT

2 x 75mm (3in) household brushes or 1 standard roller plus tray / container for mixing glaze / dragging brush or 1 x 75mm (3in) flat, long-bristled brush / rags / disposable gloves / wirewool (optional) / 1 x 50mm (2in) household brush

INSTRUCTIONS

ALWAYS WORK IN A WELL-VENTILATED AREA

Base coat

Stir the eggshell paint well and apply an even coat (see p. 34) to your prepared surface with a 75mm (3in) household brush (or roller). Allow to dry (24 hours).

Glaze coat

1 Pour the oil-based scumble into the container. Add the ultramarine, prussian blue and yellow ochre and mix well.
2 Stir in the white spirit (a little at a time) until the glaze has a milky consistency.
3 Using a 75mm (3in) household brush (or roller), apply to the base coat, working with horizontal and vertical strokes for an even texture.
4 Put on the gloves and wear for the remainder of this stage. Starting at the top of the surface, use the dragging or long-bristled brush to draw or drag the glaze down to the bottom in one uninterrupted stroke (see p. 35). Wipe the brush clean on a rag. Keeping a check on the alignment, begin another stroke. For a rougher effect, repeat the action after each stroke or once the entire wall has been dragged. Or redrag using wirewool instead of the brush (see p. 35). (Wipe the wirewool clean after each stroke.) Allow to dry (24 hours).

Protective coat

Apply one coat of dead flat varnish, using the 50mm (2in) household brush.

❶ **DEEP BLUE ON WHITE and PALE BLUE ON ULTRAMARINE** The upper section illustrates the colourway and method used in the basic recipe. The lower section appears as a mirror image of the other, but different colours are used to achieve the effect. The base coat is a premixed ultramarine eggshell paint, and the glaze tone is a mix of 2tbsp titanium white and $\frac{1}{4}$tsp ultramarine. It has been dragged and then redragged three or four times with wirewool. The border was stencilled with tinted eggshell paint.

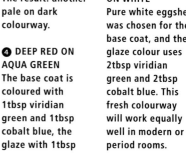

2 OCHRE ON STONE
A pale glaze dragged over a deeper base coat: a modern approach. The glaze is tinted with 2tbsp yellow ochre and 1tbsp raw umber and applied to a base coat which is coloured simply with 2tbsp yellow ochre.

3 PALE PINK ON TERRACOTTA
The base colour is a mix of 2tbsp yellow ochre and 1tbsp red oxide, and the glaze coat uses 2tbsp titanium white and 1/2tbsp cadmium red and 1/2tsp cobalt blue. The result: another pale on dark colourway.

4 DEEP RED ON AQUA GREEN
The base coat is coloured with 1tbsp viridian green and 1tbsp cobalt blue, the glaze with 1tbsp cadmium red, 1/2tbsp red oxide and 1/2tbsp burnt umber. This gives a sumptuous look.

5 SEAGREEN ON WHITE
Pure white eggshell was chosen for the base coat, and the glaze colour uses 2tbsp viridian green and 2tbsp cobalt blue. This fresh colourway will work equally well in modern or period rooms.

2

3

4

5

STIPPLING

Traditionally stippling entails the reworking of newly applied paint to create a finely textured, matt finish. Glaze brushed over a different colour or tone and stippled (as here) will reveal glimpses of the colour below. A well-prepared surface is essential – the technique emphasizes any imperfection – and oil-based paints are preferable. It also needs a steady hand. Stippling brushes give the best results; block brushes (or shoe brushes) are cheaper alternatives. An elegant effect which adds subtle ageing to a room, it also looks good on wood panelling, furniture and frames.

BASIC RECIPE – OIL-BASED RED ON RED

INGREDIENTS

Base coat ▶ 1 litre premixed deep red low-odour eggshell paint
Glaze coat ▶ 500ml premixed oil-based scumble glaze (transparent) / 3tbsp cadmium red artists' oil colour / 1/2tbsp raw umber artists' oil colour / 1tbsp linseed oil / 150ml white spirit
Protective coat ▶ 1 litre oil-based clear dead flat varnish

EQUIPMENT

2 x 75mm (3in) household brushes or 1 standard roller plus tray / container for mixing glaze / disposable gloves / stippling or block brush / rags / 1 x 50mm (2in) household brush

INSTRUCTIONS
Base coat

ALWAYS WORK IN A WELL-VENTILATED AREA

Stir the eggshell paint well and apply an even coat (see p. 34) to your prepared surface with a 75mm (3in) household brush (or roller). Allow to dry (24 hours).

Glaze coat

1 Pour the oil-based scumble into a container. Add the cadmium red and raw umber and stir well.
2 Add the linseed oil and a little white spirit and mix again. Stirring all the time, add more white spirit until you have a milky but not too runny consistency.
3 Apply to the base coat with a 75mm (3in) household brush (or clean roller), using vertical and horizontal strokes for an even finish and covering the base coat completely. If you use a brush, quickly dab the end of it over the glazed surface to get rid of any brush marks (see p. 34).
4 Put on the gloves and wear for the remainder of this stage. Lightly dab the stippling or block brush over the surface, using a gentle tapping action (see p. 35). Clean any drips with a rag. It is better to work with the wrist rather than the arm as it is less tiring and gives a softer look. Vary the finish by changing the angle of the brush from time to time. Allow to dry completely (24 hours).

Protective coat

Apply one coat of dead flat varnish, using the 50mm (2in) household brush.

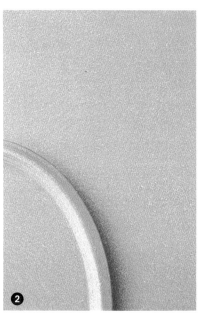

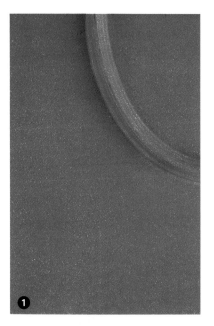

❶ RED ON RED
The basic recipe: in this classic scheme the deep red glaze appears even more intense alongside tiny flecks of the red base coat. The result is a subtle but dramatic way of executing the effect.

❷ GREEN ON GREEN
For the base coat, 1 litre white low-odour eggshell paint is tinted with 1¹/₂tbsp sap green. The glaze coat follows the basic recipe, but using 1¹/₂tbsp sap green and 1tbsp titanium white. This would be a lovely scheme for a bathroom.

❸ DEEP GREEN ON STONE
The colouring in the base coat is 2tbsp yellow ochre and ¹/₂tbsp raw sienna (stirred into 1 litre white low-odour eggshell paint). Again, the glaze follows the basic recipe, but using 2tbsp sap green and ¹/₂tbsp raw umber. These striking tones have the authority for a period setting.

❹ YELLOW ON YELLOW OCHRE
A bold colourway for a contemporary home: 1 litre white low-odour eggshell paint is coloured with 2tbsp yellow ochre to create the base, while the glaze follows the basic recipe, but using 3tbsp yellow ochre and ¹/₂tbsp cadmium yellow.

WATER-BASED STIPPLING

Apply two coats of a premixed deep red emulsion. Allow to dry (2–3 hours). Then mix a glaze using the same quantities as for the basic recipe but substituting acrylic scumble and artists' acrylic for the oil-based scumble and oil colours, and water for the linseed oil and white spirit. Apply the glaze and stipple as described opposite. Allow to dry (2–3 hours) and apply one coat of a matt or silk acrylic varnish as required. It is important to work quickly as water-based products dry faster than oil-based ones.

Right: The walls of this country kitchen have been sponged, and the cupboard doors dragged (see pp. 56 and 62). A final coat of varnish on the wood means that marking will not be a problem. Dragging is a good technique for decorating plain cupboards – the brush strokes are shorter and so much easier to control.

Left: Blue-sponged walls create an airy backdrop for a mix of antiques, modern furniture and objets d'art in this delightful bedroom (see p. 56). The simple border has been hand painted in blue and grey and is an attractive way to handle the often awkward juxtaposition of a paint-finished wall and a ceiling painted just with a solid colour.

Above: The walls above the high dado rail are stencilled chequer-board style (see p.187) in subtle tones of olive green over a paler olive base coat.

Left: Here the walls are decorated with a gentle mix of lime- and colourwashing (see pp. 52 and 68). The soft, sandy tones and instant, aged feel are lovely with the stone flooring.

LIMEWASHING

Limewash was the masonry or exterior paint of the medieval period. I have always loved that scrubbed-chalk look and devised this finish to emulate the effect using modern emulsion paints and a coloured base coat. It is easy to do and the drying time is relatively short. But it does require some hard work to reveal the ground colour. The more you rub the more authentic the surface will look. This is a versatile finish for period or modern interiors. Kitchens and garden and utility rooms are obvious choices but bathrooms and bedrooms work well too.

BASIC RECIPE – LIMEWASH ON PLASTER PINK

INGREDIENTS

Base coat ▶ 1 litre white vinyl matt emulsion / 2tbsp venetian red artists' acrylic colour / 1tbsp yellow ochre artists' acrylic colour / 1/2tbsp raw sienna artists' acrylic colour
Wash coat ▶ 1 litre white vinyl matt emulsion
Distressing the surface ▶ 250ml methylated spirits
Optional sealing coat ▶ 250ml liming wax

EQUIPMENT

Container for mixing paint / 2 x 75mm (3in) emulsion brushes / rags / protective mask / disposable gloves / soft polishing cloth (optional)

INSTRUCTIONS
Base coat

1 Pour the emulsion into the container. Add the venetian red, yellow ochre and raw sienna and stir well.
2 Apply to your prepared surface in random brush strokes (see p. 34). Allow to dry (2–3 hours).

Wash coat

1 Stir the emulsion well. Dip the tip of the other brush into the paint and wipe the excess off with a rag.
2 Using a loose wrist, brush the remaining paint onto the base coat. Recharge the brush, again wiping off the excess, and repeat. Aim for an uneven finish, applying paint more heavily in some areas and allowing some of the base coat to show through. For an even more textured look, increase the paint layers yet again. Allow to dry (2–3 hours).

Distressing the surface

Put on the mask and gloves. Moisten a rag with methylated spirits and rub it firmly over the dry surface, working some areas more vigorously than others – you are aiming for an uneven effect. Some of the paint will begin to disperse, leaving a cloudy, aged finish. Allow to dry (4 hours).

Notes Increase the aged look by using a rag to rub liming wax onto selected areas. But it will need to be buffed up with a soft polishing cloth. (It also acts as a sealant.)
Exterior use Finish with two coats of matt polyurethane varnish.

❶ LIMEWASH ON PLASTER PINK
The basic recipe: these colours suggest the traditional form of limewash, that is over a sealed, unpainted plaster wall. A rustic effect which is ideal for a farmhouse kitchen, the finish is hardwearing and performs well in such well-worked spaces.

PAINT RECIPES

2 LIMEWASH ON YELLOW
Here the emulsion base coat is tinted with 3tbsp cadmium yellow, and the standard white mock limewash is applied on top – a bright effect to try in a garden room or conservatory.

3 LIMEWASH ON LILAC
A contemporary colourway, perhaps for a bathroom. No colour mixing for the base coat this time – it is a pre-mixed deep lilac emulsion, topped with the limewash.

4 LIMEWASH ON EAU DE NIL
The base coat is tinted with 2tbsp chromium green and 1tbsp yellow ochre, and on top is the basic limewash.

DRY BRUSHING

In this technique the brush is kept relatively dry as glaze is applied lightly over a base coat to create a cloudy effect. I have used a white base coat for all these examples, but the finish is just as successful on a tinted base or when the dry-brushed coat is the lighter. It can be subtle if applied in soft tones with soft strokes or bold if you use hard-bristled brushes and strong colours. An easy way to give texture to modern interiors, it is also used to create an aged finish for period settings – scene painters often use it to age scenery and props. It is ideal for highlighting architectural mouldings and, because it is extremely resilient, for furniture.

BASIC RECIPE – DEEP BLUE ON WHITE

INGREDIENTS

Base coat ► 1 litre white vinyl matt emulsion
Glaze coat ► 250ml white vinyl matt emulsion / 250ml acrylic scumble glaze (transparent) / 3tbsp ultramarine artists' acrylic colour / 1tbsp neutral grey artists' acrylic colour / 125ml water
Optional protective coat ► 1 litre clear matt or silk acrylic varnish

EQUIPMENT

1 x 75mm (3in) emulsion brush or standard roller plus tray / container for mixing glaze / 1 x 50mm (2in) hard-bristled brush / scrap wooden board / 1 x 50mm (2in) varnish brush (optional)

INSTRUCTIONS
Base coat

Stir the emulsion well and apply an even coat (see p. 34) to your prepared surface with the 75mm (3in) brush (or roller). Allow to dry (2–3 hours).

Glaze coat

1 Pour the emulsion into the container. Add the acrylic scumble, ultramarine, neutral grey, and water (a little at a time), stirring well.
2 Dip the tip of the hard-bristled brush into the glaze and remove excess paint on the wooden board. Working with random, short brush strokes, apply to the base (see p. 34). Recharge the brush as the glaze becomes too light, still letting some of the base show through. Leave to dry (2 hours).

Notes For greater depth of colour, repeat the glazing stage, but make sure the first coat has dried first. For a hardwearing finish, apply one coat of varnish and allow to dry (2–3 hours).
Exterior use Substitute smooth masonry paint for the base coat and finish with two coats of polyurethane varnish.

Above left: This wall was dry brushed in several tones to give interest and variety. A coat of gesso before dry brushing and another of size afterwards added an aged effect. The dramatic mix of three separate glaze coats – green, lilac and purple applied in random patches and then blended together – has a modern feel that confirms an eclectic taste is at work here.

❶ DEEP BLUE ON WHITE
The basic recipe colourway: this delightful bathroom blue was dry brushed only once.

❷ YELLOW ON WHITE
Here the bright glaze is tinted with 2tbsp cadmium yellow and ¹/₂tbsp vermilion red. This is a sunny, cheering scheme that would sit extremely well in the living or dining room of either a modern or more traditional home.

❸ PEACH PINK ON WHITE
The glaze colour is a mix of 2tbsp rose madder pink and 1tbsp titanium white, spiked with ¹/₂tsp cadmium yellow for a gentle, feminine look that would work in a bedroom.

❹ BRIGHT GREEN ON WHITE
This vibrant glaze is coloured with 2tbsp chromium green and 1tbsp cadmium yellow. The resulting tone would be ideal in a kitchen or bathroom. Try it in a garden room too, where it is surprisingly effective.

FADE-AWAY WASHING

Really an extension of colourwashing, fade-away washing derives from the technique of the scene painter. I use this subtle form of shading to manipulate the dimensions of a room. A high ceiling, for example, can be lowered if you use a darker tone of your chosen colour near the ceiling, and conversely darker shading near the floor gives an illusion of height. Fade-away washing works well on poor surfaces, providing you prepare well. Plan before you begin painting – decide where your light and dark tones will be and make every wall match or the result will look very odd. Soft, neutral colours are best, and the main colour should be pale so that darker shading makes an effective contrast.

BASIC RECIPE – DARK GREY OVER DOVE GREY

INGREDIENTS

Base coat ▶ 1 litre white vinyl silk emulsion / 2tbsp neutral grey artists' acrylic colour / 1/2tbsp yellow ochre artists' acrylic colour

Dark glaze coat ▶ 250ml white vinyl silk emulsion / 125ml acrylic scumble glaze / 3tbsp burnt umber artists' acrylic colour / 2tbsp neutral grey artists' acrylic colour / 150ml water

Light glaze coat ▶ 250ml white vinyl silk emulsion / 125ml acrylic scumble glaze (transparent) / 3tbsp paynes grey artists' acrylic colour / 150ml water

Optional protective coat ▶ 1 litre clear matt acrylic varnish

EQUIPMENT

3 containers for mixing paint and glaze / 1 x 75mm (3in) emulsion brush or standard roller plus tray / 3 x 50mm (2in) emulsion brushes / rags / 1 x 50mm (2in) varnish brush (optional)

INSTRUCTIONS
Base coat

1 Pour the emulsion into one of the containers. Add the neutral grey and yellow ochre and stir well.

2 Apply an even coat (see p. 34) to your prepared surface, using the 75mm (3in) emulsion brush (or roller). Allow to dry completely (2–3 hours).

Glaze coats

1 To prepare the dark glaze: pour the emulsion into a second container, add the acrylic scumble, burnt umber, neutral grey, and water (a little at a time), and stir well.

2 To prepare the light glaze: pour the emulsion into a third container, add the acrylic scumble, paynes grey, and water (a little at a time), and stir well.

3 Using one of the 50mm (2in) emulsion brushes, apply the dark glaze with vertical strokes to approximately the top 45cm (18in) of the wall, allowing some of the base coat to show through.

4 Apply the light glaze to the remainder of the wall with a second 50mm (2in) emulsion brush, using the same vertical action.

5 Using a third, dry 50mm (2in) emulsion brush and short, overlapping, crisscross strokes, skim over the surface, gently merging the glazes into each other. Wipe excess paint off the brush with a rag to prevent clogging. Concentrate on an area no larger than 1m² (3ft²) at a time, until you have created the effect you want. Allow to dry (2–3 hours).

Notes For a hardwearing finish, apply one coat of varnish and allow to dry (2–3 hours).

❶ DARK GREY OVER DOVE GREY The basic recipe: dark shading from the ceiling down approx. 45cm (18in) before the lighter shade appears. In these tones the effect is classical.

❷ PALE YELLOW OVER DARK YELLOW Here the technique is reversed: the dark shade is used nearer the floor, adding height and depth to the room. The base coat is coloured with 2tbsp yellow ochre; the pale glaze uses 2tbsp yellow ochre and 1tbsp raw sienna, while the dark glaze adds 1¹/₂tbsp burnt umber to the pale glaze mix.

❶

❷

LOOSE-GLAZE BRUSHING

Loose-glaze brushing is a softer, looser form of dragging which I developed from period finishes I studied in stately homes of the eighteenth and early nineteenth centuries. Because the effect uses water-based paints it is simple to achieve and it dries a great deal faster than conventional dragging (see p. 62) but to give much the same pleasing results. As the technique and materials require less effort to control than in oil-based dragging you can brush the glaze horizontally or diagonally as well as vertically, which makes it a versatile finish. A large emulsion brush is the only special tool you will need and this is far cheaper than a dragging brush. Another advantage of loose-glaze brushing is that it can be used on poor surfaces. The water-based glaze is thinner and the effect you are aiming for less precise so minor imperfections tend not to show up. However, do fill any large cracks or holes to stop paint collecting there. As a resilient and hardwearing finish, loose-glaze brushing can also be used successfully on furniture.

This room has been loose-glaze brushed vertically in a soft green to give the same sense of height as vertical stripes. Although based upon period effects, the finish will adapt well to a variety of modern interiors.

BASIC RECIPE – DEEP GREEN ON MINT GREEN

INGREDIENTS

Base coat ▶ 1 litre white vinyl matt emulsion / 2tbsp viridian green artists' acrylic colour / 1tbsp brilliant green artists' acrylic colour
Glaze coat ▶ 500ml white vinyl matt emulsion / 250ml acrylic scumble glaze (transparent) / 2tbsp viridian green artists' acrylic colour / 2tbsp oxide of chromium green artists' acrylic colour / 1tbsp emerald green artists' acrylic colour / 300ml water
Optional protective coat ▶ 1 litre clear matt or silk acrylic varnish

EQUIPMENT

2 containers for mixing paint and glaze / 1 x 75mm (3in) emulsion brush or standard roller plus tray / 1 x 125mm (5in) long-bristled emulsion brush / rags / 1 x 50mm (2in) varnish brush (optional)

INSTRUCTIONS

Base coat

1 Pour the emulsion into one of the containers. Add the viridian and brilliant greens and stir well.

2 Apply evenly (see p. 34) to your prepared surface with the 75mm (3in) brush (or roller). Allow to dry (2–3 hours).

Glaze coat

1 Pour the emulsion into the other container. Add the acrylic scumble, viridian, oxide of chromium and emerald greens, and water (a little at a time), stirring well.

2 Load the 125mm (5in) brush with glaze and apply in a series of single, uninterrupted strokes, working from top to bottom of the surface and overlapping each stroke slightly.

3 Using the same brush, work over the surface again until faint brush lines appear on the glaze as you begin to drag it. Eradicate any drips with a rag. Allow to dry (2 hours).

Notes For a hardwearing finish, apply one coat of varnish and allow to dry (2–3 hours).

❶ DEEP GREEN ON MINT GREEN
The basic, traditional colourway, but with diagonal brush strokes to suggest an engaging alternative. The effect is loose and free without being sloppy.

❷ STONE ON BLUE
Here a pale glaze has been applied to a premixed deep blue emulsion base. The strokes are horizontal. The glaze colour-mix is 2tbsp titanium white, 1/2tbsp raw sienna and 1/2tbsp yellow ochre.

❸ PALE PINK ON RED
This example, with vertical brushing, recalls the classic dragged look. The glaze is coloured with 2tbsp titanium white, 2tbsp cadmium red and 1/2tbsp rose madder pink and applied to a base of premixed deep red emulsion.

SIMPLE FRESCO

This finish gives the look often seen in old Italian frescos, where medieval painters perfected a technique which involved the application of water-based colours to wet plaster. Thankfully my recipe does not have to be applied to newly plastered walls – it just looks as if it does. Most authentic when undertaken in the colours of true fresco, this hardwearing effect is ideal for walls and ceilings and resilient enough for kitchens and bathrooms. A good way of ageing new interiors, it is also an excellent backdrop for stencilling. Plaster mouldings and other architectural details respond well to the technique too, and you can perform miracles with old furniture and frames.

BASIC RECIPE – TERRACOTTA ON CORAL

INGREDIENTS

Base coat ▶ 1 litre white vinyl matt emulsion / 2tbsp venetian red artists' acrylic colour / ¹/₂tbsp raw sienna artists' acrylic colour
Glaze coat ▶ 500ml white vinyl matt emulsion / 250ml acrylic scumble glaze (transparent) / 2tbsp bronze ochre artists' acrylic colour / 2tbsp raw sienna artists' acrylic colour / ¹/₂tbsp venetian red artists' acrylic colour / 250ml water
Distressing the surface ▶ 1 x 500ml tin liming wax / 50g (1³/₄oz) whiting or chalk powder

EQUIPMENT

2 containers for mixing paint and glaze / 1 x 75mm (3in) emulsion brush / 1 x 50mm (2in) hard-bristled brush / disposable gloves / rags / water for soaking rags / medium-grade sandpaper

INSTRUCTIONS
Base coat

1 Pour the emulsion into one of the containers. Add the venetian red and raw sienna, and stir well.
2 Apply to your prepared surface with the emulsion brush, using random strokes (see p. 34). Allow to dry (2–3 hours).

Glaze coat

1 Pour the emulsion into the other container. Add the acrylic scumble, bronze ochre, raw sienna, venetian red, and water (a little at a time), and stir well.
2 Apply to the base coat, using the hard-bristled brush. Work in all directions, using rough, uneven brush strokes.
3 Wear gloves for all the remaining stages. Quickly immerse a rag in water and wring it out until almost dry. Use the damp rag to rub the glaze into the base coat with a circular motion, varying the effect as much as possible. Allow to dry (1 hour).

Distressing the surface

1 Rub sandpaper over the surface in some areas to remove some of the paint.

Above left: Here the simple fresco technique has been applied to a plaster-cast head of Dante, using the archetypal terracotta on coral colourway of the basic recipe. Note how rubbing whiting into the surface has taken off some of the colour.

2 Rub liming wax into other areas on a clean rag.

3 Again using a clean rag, quickly rub a little whiting into the waxed areas to create a dusty effect.

Notes If you want a greater depth of colour, repeat the glazing and sandpapering sequences before you begin steps 2–3 of Distressing the surface.

Exterior use Substitute smooth masonry paint in the base coat and finish with two coats of matt polyurethane varnish.

❶ TERRACOTTA ON CORAL
On a flat surface the basic colour-way seems to gain intensity. This is a rich scheme for a grand neoclassical living room.

❷ COBALT BLUE ON STONE
The base coat is tinted with 1tbsp raw sienna and 1tbsp burnt umber, and the glaze with 3tbsp cobalt blue and 1tbsp prussian blue for a colour popular in medieval frescos.

❸ GREEN ON STONE
This bright variation is an experiment in modern colours. The base coat is made as for sample 2, while the glaze colour-mix is 3tbsp bright green with 1tbsp yellow ochre.

❹ SALMON PINK ON STONE
Another fresco scheme, this would suit modern or period rooms. The stone base of sample 2 softens a glaze tinted with 2tbsp rose madder pink, 1/2tbsp titanium white and 1/2tsp yellow ochre.

MEDITERRANEAN

Think of Mediterranean countries and you are sure to conjure up the wonderful chalky colours of sunbaked, painted houses. These are paint mixes and methods of application that have developed over centuries, some of them typical of a particular region or country. Poor areas are sometimes forced to dilute paint to make it go further, while milk powders and chalk are also used to supplement precious pigments, so the extraordinary depth of colour we associate with such lands is due often to a build-up of paint layers as a protection against the elements. I developed this finish to simulate the look and colours of the Mediterranean palette. Random brushing and hard rubbing create the characteristic roughness and depth of tone. It can be used on a variety of surfaces but is naturally suited to uneven plaster and textured surfaces, both inside and out. Try it on simple wooden furniture too.

BASIC RECIPE – VENETIAN GREEN

INGREDIENTS

Gesso coat ► 1 litre white acrylic gesso
Base coat ► 1 litre white vinyl matt emulsion
Glaze coats ► 500ml white vinyl matt emulsion / 500ml acrylic scumble glaze (transparent) / 2tbsp emerald green artists' acrylic colour / 2tbsp brilliant green artists' acrylic colour / 1tbsp cobalt green artists' acrylic colour / 200ml water (approx.)
Optional protective coat ► 1 litre clear matt acrylic varnish

EQUIPMENT

3 x 75mm (3in) emulsion brushes / container for mixing glaze / rags / disposable gloves / 1 x 50mm (2in) varnish brush (optional)

INSTRUCTIONS
Gesso coat

Stir the acrylic gesso well and apply to your entire prepared surface, using random brush strokes (see p. 34) to create a resilient texture. Allow to dry (1 hour).

Base coat

Stir the emulsion well and brush an even coat (see p. 34) onto the gesso. Allow to dry (2–3 hours).

Glaze coats

1 Pour the emulsion into the container. Add the acrylic scumble, emerald, brilliant and cobalt greens, and water (a little at a time), stirring well until you have a creamy but not runny consistency.
2 Apply half the glaze to the surface in random brush strokes. Try to vary the thickness of the glaze in some areas, and allow some of the base coat to show through in others.
3 Put on the gloves. Using a rag, rub the glaze into the surface. You are aiming for a rough effect so work some areas more thoroughly than others. Allow to dry (2–3 hours).
4 Using the remaining glaze, repeat steps 2–3, and again allow to dry (2–3 hours).

Opposite: A delightful yellow stairway which seems to lead the sunshine indoors. Yellow is a popular choice for interiors in Spain, Italy and France. Try it in garden rooms, where it will complement the greens of foliage plants.

❶ VENETIAN GREEN
The basic recipe: a colour often seen in the islands of the Venetian lagoon. Its bright, airy look suits many rooms. In all these samples glimpses of the white base make for an authentically chalky appearance. But here the green has been rubbed back a little with sandpaper to reveal more of the white base coat.

❷ TUSCAN ORANGE
This orange, the colour of exterior walls through much of Italy, works well in kitchens. The glaze colour is 2tbsp yellow ochre, 1tbsp raw umber and 1/2tbsp cadmium red.

❸ PROVENÇAL PINK
From the south of France: 3tbsp titanium white, 1 1/2tbsp rose madder pink and 1/2tbsp magenta tint the glaze in a pretty bedroom or bathroom choice.

❹ AEGEAN BLUE
This glorious Greek blue is made with a mix of 2tbsp ultramarine and 1tbsp cobalt blue. Ideal for a modern setting, it would go well in a bathroom.

Notes The more this finish is worked the more authentic it is. Repeat the glazing stage several times to build up the colour, but some of the base coat must show through. Dry brushing (see p. 70) also adds to the effect. Or use medium-grade sandpaper to rub the dry glaze back a little. Acrylic scumble and gesso create a tough finish, but for very hard wear apply one coat of varnish and allow to dry (2–3 hours).

Exterior use Substitute masonry paint for the base coat and finish with two coats of matt polyurethane varnish.

E G Y P T I A N

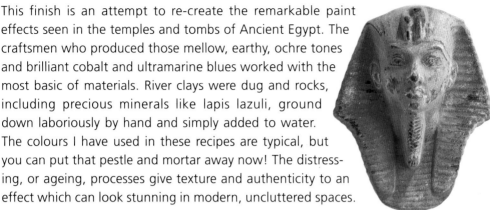

This finish is an attempt to re-create the remarkable paint effects seen in the temples and tombs of Ancient Egypt. The craftsmen who produced those mellow, earthy, ochre tones and brilliant cobalt and ultramarine blues worked with the most basic of materials. River clays were dug and rocks, including precious minerals like lapis lazuli, ground down laboriously by hand and simply added to water. The colours I have used in these recipes are typical, but you can put that pestle and mortar away now! The distressing, or ageing, processes give texture and authenticity to an effect which can look stunning in modern, uncluttered spaces.

BASIC RECIPE – LAPIS BLUE ON OCHRE

INGREDIENTS

Base coat ▶ 1 litre white vinyl matt emulsion / 3tbsp yellow ochre artists' acrylic colour / 1tbsp raw sienna artists' acrylic colour

First glaze coat ▶ 250ml white vinyl matt emulsion / 500ml acrylic scumble glaze (transparent) / 3tbsp burnt umber artists' acrylic colour / 2tbsp venetian red artists' acrylic colour / 2tbsp yellow ochre artists' acrylic colour / 200ml water

Second glaze coat ▶ 500ml white vinyl matt emulsion / 4tbsp ultramarine artists' acrylic colour / 2tbsp cobalt blue artists' acrylic colour / 150ml water

Distressing the surface ▶ 125ml methylated spirits / 50g (1³/₄oz) whiting or chalk powder

EQUIPMENT

4 containers for mixing paint and glaze, and for whiting / 3 x 75mm (3in) emulsion brushes / large, well-worn, hard-bristled brush / disposable gloves / rags / water to dampen the surface / medium-grade sandpaper

INSTRUCTIONS

Base coat

1 Pour the emulsion into one of the containers. Add the yellow ochre and raw sienna, and stir well.

2 Using one of the 75mm (3in) emulsion brushes, apply to your prepared surface with random brush strokes (see p. 34) and allow to dry (2–3 hours).

First glaze coat

1 Pour the emulsion into a second container. Add the acrylic scumble, burnt umber, venetian red, yellow ochre, and water (a little at a time), and stir well.

2 Apply the glaze with a second 75mm (3in) emulsion brush, using random brush strokes and allowing some of the base coat to show through.

3 Working with the dry, hard-bristled brush, go quickly over the glazed surface (see p. 34). Once again your brush strokes should be random – your aim is to roughen the effect and reveal more of the base coat. Allow to dry (1–2 hours).

Above: I used a premixed deep burgundy emulsion for this irresistible plaster head, while for the glaze colour I used 2tbsp ultramarine and 1tbsp cobalt blue. Some areas were sanded back to add age, and extra whiting was applied to highlight the detail.

① LAPIS BLUE ON OCHRE
The basic colour-way with added texture. A layer of plaster was applied roughly to the surface, and a ruler 2.5cm (1in) wide was used to incise the decoration while the plaster was still wet. It was allowed to dry for 24 hours before painting began.

② BURGUNDY ON CORAL
The base coat is a premixed coral emulsion, and the glaze colour-mix uses 2tbsp cadmium red, 1/2tbsp burnt umber and 1/4tbsp dioxazine purple. This is an opulent scheme which works well with antiques and ethnic ornaments.

③ OCHRE ON SAND
Earthy, strong colours that would sit easily in living and dining rooms: the base colour is a mixture of 3tbsp yellow ochre and 1/2tbsp red oxide; the glaze is tinted with 3tbsp yellow ochre, 1/2tbsp red oxide and 1/2tbsp raw umber.

Second glaze coat

1 Pour the emulsion into a third container. Add the ultra-marine, cobalt blue, and water (a little at a time) and stir well. **2** Dipping only the tip of a third 75mm (3in) emulsion brush into the paint, apply to the surface with rough brush strokes. You are aiming for an uneven coverage to create a 'cloudy' effect. The deep blue paint should be heavily applied in some areas, and much more lightly in others – and leave the first glaze and base coats to show through in places. Allow to dry (1–2 hours). If you want to produce an even deeper blue, repeat this stage before you begin ageing, or distressing, the surface, as described opposite.

Distressing the surface

1 Put on the gloves and wear throughout this stage. Dip a rag in methylated spirits and wipe it over the entire surface. This will cause the paint to begin breaking down in some areas, leaving only a thin film of colour behind. Allow to dry (2–3 hours).

2 Place the whiting (or chalk powder) in a fourth container. Moisten the entire surface with a damp rag and, using the same rag, add a thin film of whiting to create an authentic chalky effect. Allow to dry (2–3 hours).

3 To age further, rub gently with sandpaper to reveal some of the paint layers below.

These walls have been painted in a style similar to the technique described here. The rich red-oxide colour and heavily aged look are an excellent backdrop for hangings and antiques.

MOCK PLASTER

This *faux* finish, with its look of aged paint brushed onto rough plaster, was reputedly first used in French café-bars of the 1970s. In fact, the broken-colour effect requires a conventional emulsion base, topped with a mix of whiting and powder pigment rubbed into a layer of wax. You can adapt this recipe to use subtle earth tones, but experimenting with bright colours is fun and the real delight of working with pigment is the intensity of colour you can achieve. Remember, though, that the strength of pigment colour can be alarming on first view so run several tests before you begin painting. Pigment colours also need thorough mixing; if you want to tone them down with more whiting, make sure you avoid streaking. The finish works best on a white base but tints can be used successfully: remember it must be acrylic colour for the water-based emulsion. Mock plaster will suit new or old interiors, and the waxed surface makes it easy to wipe clean. Try it on garden ornaments too, especially those made of plaster.

A mock-plaster finish can add interest to plaster mouldings and other architectural details. Here I used cadmium green to highlight a standard ceiling rose.

BASIC RECIPE – ULTRAMARINE ON WHITE

INGREDIENTS
Base coats ▶ 2 litres white vinyl matt emulsion
Top coat ▶ 1 x 500ml tub white wax / 250g (8³/₄oz) ultramarine powder pigment / 250g (8³/₄oz) whiting or chalk powder
Optional protective coat ▶ 1 litre clear matt acrylic varnish

EQUIPMENT
1 x 75mm (3in) emulsion brush or standard roller plus tray /rags / protective mask / small container for mixing pigment / 1 x 50mm (2in) varnish brush (optional)

INSTRUCTIONS
Base coats
Stir the emulsion well and apply two even coats (see p. 34) to your prepared surface, using the brush (or roller). Allow 2–3 hours for each coat to dry.

Top coat
1 Using a rag and a circular action, rub a thick but even layer of white wax into the base coat.
2 Put on the mask. Place the ultramarine and whiting (or chalk powder) in the container and stir well.
3 Using another rag, rub the whiting mixture quickly into the wax with a downward action to give a broken colour finish very like real plaster. Allow to dry completely (2–3 hours).

Notes Repeat the top coat with another colour to vary the effect. For a hardwearing finish, apply one coat of varnish and allow to dry (2–3 hours).
Exterior use Add a coat of wax polish after the top coat, and finish with a coat of satin polyurethane varnish.

❶ ULTRAMARINE ON WHITE
The basic recipe: this strong colour is ideal for a bathroom, where mock plaster's wipe-clean qualities would be appreciated.

❷ PINK ON WHITE
Three powder pigments are used to create a dramatic pink for the top coat: 125g (4²/₅oz) alizarin crimson and 100g (3¹/₂oz) magenta, sharpened with 25g (⁹/₁₀oz) ultramarine. Follow the basic recipe for the base coats.

❸ OCHRE ON WHITE
A sample to demonstrate the use of pure yellow ochre pigment in the top coat (quantity as for the basic recipe). This stunning variation would look delightful in a traditional interior. Again, follow the basic recipe for the base coats.

Left: Loose-glaze brushing in red on a red ground for a highly dramatic statement. This modern effect (see p. 74), derived from the French eigheenth-century art of dragging, and the choice of colour pay graceful compliment to the heavy doors and handsome panelling of a period home.

Above: Umber and sand tones are used for an authentic fresco look (see p. 76). The script high on the wall is a painterly touch.

Left: The walls are subtly washed in several colours (see p. 52) over a gesso base; a final coat of size seals the finish. The deeper tones below shoulder height lend substance to the scheme.

Right: A great example of the modern look you can create with bold pigment colour and a mock-plaster finish (see p. 84).

RUBBED-BACK PLASTER

This technique illustrates another way of instantly ageing a new surface. It is a simple, traditional look inspired by the roughly painted walls I have seen in unrestored artisan cottages of the late nineteenth and early twentieth centuries. Money and time were limited so, when the inhabitants fancied a change of decoration, they often painted straight over the previous colour in a single coat, sometimes making the paint stretch further by applying it sparingly to the surface or by diluting it with water.

The effect is achieved by adding whiting or chalk powder to contrasting glazes to age them, by applying the paint roughly with hard-bristled brushes and by rubbing down each colour with sandpaper. The result is a similar, but softer, finish to that seen in limewashing (see p. 68), and the colour combinations are built on gentle, undemanding pastels which give depth and interest to a surface.

Rubbed-back plaster is a versatile effect which establishes an essentially informal look that seems to work especially well in kitchens. Try it in a bathroom with woodwashed pine if you are lucky enough to have an old, cast-iron bath. It is a good-tempered finish and, as ageing is so much part of its charm, it only benefits from any knocks it receives.

BASIC RECIPE – AQUAMARINE ON PALE PINK

INGREDIENTS

Base coat ▶ 1 litre white vinyl matt emulsion
First colour ▶ 250ml white vinyl matt emulsion / 125ml rose madder pink artists' acrylic colour / 100g (3^1/2oz) whiting or chalk powder / 125ml water
Second colour ▶ 250ml white vinyl matt emulsion / 4tbsp turquoise blue artists' acrylic colour / 2tbsp bright green artists' acrylic colour / 1tbsp cobalt blue artists' acrylic colour / 100g (3^1/2oz) whiting or chalk powder / 125ml water
Optional protective coat ▶ 1 litre clear matt acrylic varnish

EQUIPMENT

1 x 75mm (3in) emulsion brush or standard roller plus tray / 2 containers for mixing colours / 2 x 75mm (3in) hard-bristled brushes / disposable gloves / medium-grade sandpaper / 1 x 50mm (2in) varnish brush (optional)

INSTRUCTIONS
Base coat

Stir the emulsion well and apply an even coat (see p. 34) to your prepared surface, using the 75mm (3in) emulsion brush (or roller). Allow to dry (2–3 hours).

First colour

1 Pour the emulsion into one of the containers and add rose madder pink, whiting (or chalk powder), and water (a little at a time), stirring well.
2 Using one of the hard-bristled brushes, apply to the base coat in random strokes (see p. 34). Allow to dry (2–3 hours).
3 Put on the gloves and rub sandpaper gently over the surface to reveal some of the base coat.

PAINT RECIPES

❶ AQUAMARINE ON PALE PINK
The basic recipe: this subtle finish has a cloudy, aged look which is extremely appealing. The colourway would suit a bathroom or bedroom.

❷ PALE GREEN ON OLIVE
The first colour here is a deep, pre-mixed olive green, and the top colour simply 250ml white vinyl matt emulsion, tinted with 1tbsp viridian green. Follow the basic recipe for quantities of whiting and water.

❸ CREAMY WHITE ON YELLOW
A bright scheme for a kitchen, living or dining room: 2tbsp cadmium yellow is used to tint the first colour coat, with a dash ($^{1}/_{2}$tbsp) of raw umber for the top coat.

❹ WARM GREY ON WHITE
This gentle colourway could be used in modern or period homes. The first colour coat is pure white, while the second is tinted with 2tbsp neutral grey and $^{1}/_{2}$tbsp yellow ochre.

RUBBED-BACK PLASTER

Second colour

1 Pour the emulsion into the other container. Add the turquoise, green, cobalt blue and whiting (or chalk powder), and mix. Then add the water (a little at a time), stirring well.

2 Using the other hard-bristled brush, apply to the first colour in random strokes. Allow to dry (2–3 hours).

3 Again rub sandpaper vigorously over the surface. Your aim is to reveal some of the first colour and base coat.

Notes For a hardwearing finish, apply one coat of varnish and allow to dry (2–3 hours).

Exterior use Substitute smooth masonry paint for the base coat and finish with two coats of matt polyurethane varnish.

A gentle, rubbed-back plaster effect is put to good use in a sitting room, proving how versatile this finish can be. The eau de nil on white scheme is reminiscent of Wedgwood, and looks lovely with antique furniture and paintings.

Painted borders are a neglected way of bringing additional interest to wall surfaces. Most often applied at chair- or picture-rail height, they can star – helping to alter the dimensions of a room by shifting the visual focus – or play a supporting role in a colour scheme. I believe that the reintroduction of paper and stencilled borders in the 1980s is beginning to rekindle an awareness of the design potential in painted borders. After all, paper borders are relatively expensive, the range of colours and patterns limited. And the sheer effort involved in stencilling a large room can leave the energetically-challenged among us wilting.

In contrast, borders painted by hand are essentially individual. You can choose the colours and patterns you want, and you can make them as simple, or as complex, as you wish. They can be primitive to fit in with an ethnic interior or draw on more classical themes for a period setting. Simple freehand designs have been used in the peasant communities of Mexico, Spain and Greece for generations, and these, and more sophisticated ideas, can be gleaned and adapted from any number of art reference books. I drew inspiration from the work of the Dutch painter Piet Mondrian for the blocks of colour which feature in the second sample, and that drew me by association to tartan.

BASIC RECIPE – SIMPLE STRIPES

INGREDIENTS	Denim blue stripe ▶ 250ml white vinyl matt emulsion / 2tbsp ultramarine artists' acrylic colour / 1tbsp prussian blue artists' acrylic colour / $^1/_2$tbsp neutral grey artists' acrylic colour Burgundy stripes ▶ 250ml white vinyl matt emulsion / 3tbsp cadmium red artists' acrylic colour / 1tbsp burnt umber artists' acrylic colour / $^1/_2$tbsp ultramarine blue artists' acrylic colour
EQUIPMENT	Metre or yard stick / set square / pencil / 2.5cm (1in) masking tape /cloth / 2 containers for paint / large and small stencil brushes / soft eraser
INSTRUCTIONS Planning the border	1 Borders are always painted after the rest of the surface, but you must plan and mark them out on the prepared surface before the rest of the wall is painted. Measure the distance from the skirting board to the required height. Using the metre/yard stick and set square, mark the appropriate height at regular intervals along the surface and use the metre/yard stick to draw a horizontal pencil line joining all the marks together. 2 Mark and draw a second line 2.5cm (1in) above the first, and a third line 2.5cm (1in) above the second, using the same method. 3 Mark and draw a fourth line 10cm (4in) above the third. 4 Mark and draw the final two lines: the fifth 2.5cm (1in) above the fourth and the sixth 2.5cm (1in) above the fifth.

BORDERS

A charming hand-painted border in a Californian home, profoundly influenced by Mexican decoration. It has been applied to a roughly textured surface and then sanded back to give it extra authenticity.

Blue stripe

1 Use masking tape to protect the 2.5cm (1in) strips immediately above and below the wider (blue) stripe. (Always remember to remove some of the tackiness from the tape by dabbing it on a cloth before using it. This prevents it from stripping paint off the surface when removed later.)

2 Pour the emulsion into one of the containers. Add the ultramarine, prussian blue and neutral grey, and stir well.

3 Dip the very end of the large stencil brush into the paint and apply it to the area between the strips of masking tape, using a firm stippling action (see p. 35). Take care not to go over the tape and onto the wall. Allow to dry (1 hour).

Burgundy stripes

1 Use additional strips of masking tape to protect the surfaces immediately above the upper stripe and below the lower one.

2 Pour the emulsion into the other container. Add the cadmium red, burnt umber and ultramarine blue, and stir well.

3 Use the small stencil brush to stipple paint onto the two narrow stripes, taking care not to go over the tape or the wide stripe. Allow to dry (1 hour) and then remove all the masking tape carefully.

4 Gently rub off any stray pencil marks.

❶ SIMPLE STRIPES
The basic recipe: the broken-colour effect of stippling softens the stripes while creating a brisk compliment to the blue wall finish. Remember that borders can be at any height and any width. Just make sure that the same height and measurements are maintained all round the room so your borders align.

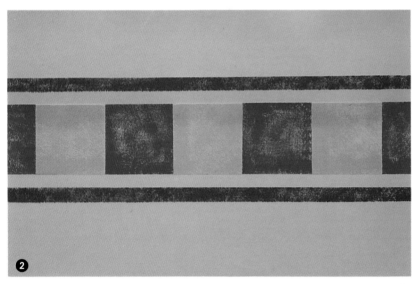

❷ STRIPES AND BLOCKS
Here quantities for the blue stripe were halved, and 2tbsp yellow ochre added to 125ml white vinyl matt emulsion to make the third colour. Alternate 10cm (4in) blocks of the wide stripe were masked with tape, the ochre stippled on, and allowed to dry (1 hour), before the ochre was masked and blue stippled on.

❸ TARTAN
A grid of horizontals and verticals in burgundy and forest green – 2tbsp sap green and ¹/₂tbsp burnt umber to 125ml white emulsion – create a new design. Narrow verticals were masked off and stippled, then the horizontals. Last to be painted were the wider verticals beside the blocks of colour. Do make sure each colour is dry before painting over it.

STONE BLOCKING

This *faux* effect is an amusing and theatrical way of making a room, hallway or entrance appear grand and imposing. It is a lengthy process, incorporating several different techniques, including stippling, veining and some decorative painting to give the appearance of line and shadow. But it is relatively simple if you use suitable equipment. Search out references for the architectural form you want to create – it will look all the more authentic if you paint what a mason would have built. It is also wise to make sure that your blocks are the right scale for your room as they can look very silly when too large or too small for the space.

BASIC RECIPE – WATER-BASED TRADITIONAL METHOD

INGREDIENTS

Base coat ▶ 1 litre white vinyl matt emulsion / 3tbsp burnt umber artists' acrylic colour

Medium glaze coat ▶ 250ml white vinyl matt emulsion / 125ml acrylic scumble glaze (transparent) / 2tbsp raw umber artists' acrylic colour / 1tbsp yellow ochre artists' acrylic colour / 150ml water

Dark glaze coat ▶ 250ml white vinyl matt emulsion / 125ml acrylic scumble glaze (transparent) / 3tbsp raw umber artists' acrylic colour / 1tbsp raw sienna artists' acrylic colour / 150ml water

Pale glaze coat ▶ 250ml white vinyl matt emulsion / 125ml acrylic scumble glaze (transparent) / 1tbsp raw umber artists' acrylic colour / 150ml water

Veining ▶ 250ml acrylic scumble glaze / 2tbsp neutral grey artists' acrylic colour / 100ml water

Shadows ▶ 3tbsp burnt umber artists' acrylic colour / 1tbsp water

Optional protective coat ▶ 1 litre clear matt acrylic varnish

EQUIPMENT

5 large and 1 small container for mixing paint and glaze / 1 x 75mm (3in) emulsion brush / T-square / ruler or straight edge / pencil or chalk / 12mm (1/2in) masking tape / cloth / soft eraser / 3 x 50mm (2in) emulsion brushes / stippling or block brushes, in various sizes / small sea sponge / water to dampen sponge / flat artists' brush / 1 x 50mm (2in) varnish brush (optional)

❶ TRADITIONAL STONE BLOCKING The basic recipe: note especially the narrow drop shadows painted in by hand between the blocks to give a three-dimensional quality. In this instance the light source is to the right. The remaining, unpainted areas of base coat provide the highlights.

A lovely example of stone blocking, used most unusually in a bathroom. Here the effect of bevelling has been introduced by the subtle use of drop shadows and highlights.

INSTRUCTIONS
Base coat

1 Pour the emulsion into one of the containers. Add the burnt umber and stir well.
2 Using the 75mm (3in) emulsion brush, apply evenly (see p. 34) to your prepared surface. Allow to dry (2–3 hours).

Marking out the blocks

1 Using the T-square and the ruler (or straight edge), mark the blocks out onto the wall with a light pencil (or chalk) line.
2 Mark out again, this time using masking tape. Make sure the tape lies flush to the lines to ensure that the blocks are all the same size and place it consistently either above or below the lines. (It is wise to remove most of the tackiness from the tape by dabbing it on a cloth before sticking it to the wall.)
3 Rub out any pencil guidelines, taking care not to disturb the tape. (Paint does not adhere well to pencil marks.)

Medium glaze coat

1 Pour the emulsion into a second container. Add the acrylic scumble, raw umber, yellow ochre, and water (a little at a time). Stir well.
2 Apply the glaze evenly to the entire surface with one of the 50mm (2in) emulsion brushes, working down the wall in vertical rows of blocks.
3 Again working down the wall, quickly dab a stippling or block brush onto the glaze with a light, tapping action (see

p. 35). Move your wrist rather than the entire arm – it is less tiring and gives a softer finish. You can also vary the finish by altering the position of your wrist. and the brush size. Allow to dry (1–2 hours).

Dark glaze coat

1 Pour the emulsion into a third container. Add the acrylic scumble, raw umber, raw sienna, and water (a little at a time), and stir well.

2 Using a second 50mm (2in) emulsion brush, apply to the entire surface and then quickly stipple the glaze as before, this time working in horizontal rows. Again vary the wrist position and brush size. Allow to dry (1–2 hours).

Pale glaze coat

1 Pour the emulsion into a fourth container. Add the acrylic scumble, raw umber, and water (a little at a time), and stir well.

2 Using a third 50mm (2in) emulsion brush, apply the glaze to the previous tones in the same way, again working horizontally, and stipple. Allow to dry (1–2 hours).

Veining

1 Pour the acrylic scumble into a fifth container. Add the neutral grey and water (a little at a time). Stir well.

2 Using a clean, damp sponge, make short, soft, diagonal lines on the surface. Each block must appear to be separate so do not draw veins over the masking tape. Allow to dry (1/2 hour), and carefully remove the masking tape.

Shadows

1 Place the burnt umber in the small container and add most of the water (a little at a time), stirring well.

2 Before beginning to paint in the shadows, decide whether the light source is to be to the left or right of the painted surface – choose a real window if possible. Part of the space between each block will be light, and part will be dark.

3 If your light source is to the left, then the right-hand side of each vertical space will be light; so will the lower part of each horizontal space (see p. 94). Using the flat artists' brush, apply a freehand line of colour (or shadow) to the left-hand halves of all the vertical spaces and the upper halves of all the horizontal spaces.

If the light source is to the right, then the light/shade relationship is reversed. Apply the shadow to the right-hand halves of all the vertical spaces and the upper halves of all the horizontal spaces. Allow to dry (1/2 hour).

Notes Apply one coat of varnish if you want a hardwearing finish and allow to dry (2–3 hours).

DISTRESSED PLASTER

The wanton distressing and staining of a recently plastered wall – to make it look, quite frankly, as if you need the decorators in – might seem a perverse thing to do, but that air of decay and decadence now has for many a certain *fin-de-siècle* charm. And if you introduce a contrasting base coat, as here, the effect can be striking. Do consider the implications carefully first, however: this is not a technique for the faint-hearted. You do not have to be a master plasterer but skill and confidence are necessary, and it is better to enlist the help of someone else if you lack either. Of course, if you want to decorate a room where the plaster is already in need of repair, a coloured base coat in the broken areas and simple staining could provide a dramatic solution.

BASIC RECIPE – STAINED GOLD ON GREEN

INGREDIENTS

Base coats ▶ 2 litres premixed sea-green vinyl matt emulsion
Sealing coat ▶ 1 litre PVA adhesive or white glue / 750ml water
Plastering ▶ 1 x 500ml tub furniture wax (clear) / 1kg (2^1/$_5$lb) multi-finish plaster / water (according to plaster manufacturer's instructions)
Staining ▶ 125ml PVA adhesive or white glue / 50g (1^3/$_4$oz) yellow ochre powder pigment / 50g (1^3/$_4$oz) burnt umber powder pigment / 50g (1^3/$_4$oz) raw sienna powder pigment / 4tbsp water

EQUIPMENT

4 x 75mm (3in) emulsion brushes or 3 brushes and 1 standard roller plus tray / dustsheets / 3 containers for mixing paint, sealant and stainer / disposable gloves / plasterer's float / hammer or bolster / scraper or spatula / medium-grade sandpaper / rags

INSTRUCTIONS
Base coats

Apply two even coats (see p. 34) to your prepared surface with a brush (or roller). Allow 2–3 hours for each coat to dry.

Sealing coat

1 Protect the surrounding area with dustsheets.
2 Pour the PVA adhesive (or white glue) into one of the containers and add the water (a little at a time), stirring well.
3 Put on the gloves and wear for all remaining stages. Using a brush, apply to the base coat and allow to dry (3 hours).

Plastering

1 Using another brush, dab furniture wax onto the areas you want to distress. It is a good idea to draw a sketch plan showing the waxed areas at this point – it will be a useful reminder when you come to distress the new plaster.
2 Quickly (before the wax dries) mix the plaster with water in a second container according to the manufacturer's instructions and apply a thin coat to the entire surface in wide, arc-like movements, using the plasterer's float. The plaster also dries quickly so brush water onto any ridges and smooth out immediately, again using the float. Allow to dry (24 hours).

DISTRESSED PLASTER

**❶ STAINED GOLD
ON GREEN**
A bold contrast in
the basic recipe
colourway: the
earth tones of the
staining soften the
sea-green base. In
all three samples
the broken edges
have been sanded
hard for a very
smooth effect.

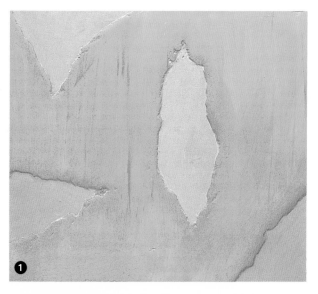

**❷ STAINED PINK
ON TERRACOTTA**
This contemporary
variation uses a
premixed terra-
cotta emulsion
base coat, while
just 25g ($^9/_{10}$oz)
alizarin crimson
powder pigment
colours the stain.

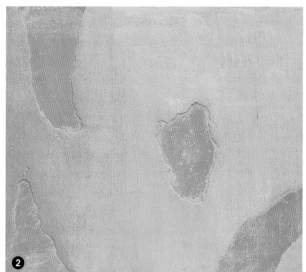

**❸ STAINED PLASTER
ON BLUE**
Here the staining
coat is left untinted
for a much softer
effect. The bright
base coat is a pre-
mixed sky blue
emulsion. Try this
version in a bath-
room perhaps.

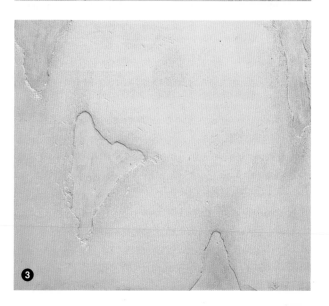

Distressing the plaster

1 Using the hammer (or bolster) and referring to your sketch plan, gently tap the areas you want to break down until you crack the plaster.

2 Carefully remove the cracked sections. The scraper (or spatula) will help you take off any stubborn pieces.

3 Rub the broken areas with sandpaper and clean the edges with rags.

Staining

1 Pour the PVA adhesive (or white glue) into a third container. Add the yellow ochre, burnt umber, raw sienna, and water (a little at a time) and stir well.

2 Apply to the new plaster with another brush, using random brush strokes. Allow to dry (2–3 hours).

Notes You can stain new plaster with the same mix – a huge range of powder pigments is available.

A staining on distressed plaster finish has heightened the atmosphere in this interior to create a less conventional setting for antique furniture and modern accessories.

TEXTURING

There are many different ways to texture paint. You can add sawdust for a coarse grain or whiting for subtlety – here I use fine sand in the base coat for a medium-grade finish. The way you apply your mix can give surface interest too. The obvious advantage of texturing is that it is a wonderful disguise for imperfect walls. But it can bring character to any surface, or a tough finish to a garden room or exterior wall. Premixed textured paints are now available in a wider colour range, although in most cases it is more satisfactory to mix your own using artists' acrylics, and the brighter tones make this simple technique remarkably versatile. The samples here use a white base as it best illustrates the finish. But the emulsion can be tinted before sand is added. Try texturing garden ornaments: statues and pots take on an antique look when a textured base is used under a rust, verdigris or lead finish (see pp.160–5).

Textured finishes inside and out: a bold, contemporary use of colour and surface interest have combined to make this an excellent choice for a minimalist home in Mexico.

BASIC RECIPE – YELLOW OCHRE ON WHITE

INGREDIENTS

Base coat ▶ 1 litre white vinyl matt emulsion / 250g (8³/₄oz) fine sand
Glaze coat ▶ 250ml white vinyl matt emulsion / 250ml acrylic scumble glaze (transparent) / 2tbsp yellow ochre artists' acrylic colour / 1tbsp raw sienna artists' acrylic colour / 150ml water
Optional protective coat ▶ 1 litre clear matt acrylic varnish

EQUIPMENT

2 containers for mixing paint and glaze / 2 x 75mm (3in) emulsion brushes / 1 x 50mm (2in) varnish brush (optional)

❶ YELLOW OCHRE ON WHITE
The basic recipe colourway, demonstrating two different textures above and below a dado rail colourwashed (see p. 52) in purple. More sand (360g or 12³/₄oz) was added to the base coat used on the lower panel to create a distinctly heavier texture.

❷ SOFT GREY ON WHITE
This sample illustrates the potential subtlety of the finish. A little very fine sand (115g or 4oz) was used in the base coat to create the gentle texturing, and 2tbsp neutral grey and ¹/₂tbsp magenta coloured the glaze.

❸ ROSE ON WHITE
A strong colour for a modern interior: the glaze is tinted with 3tbsp magenta and 1tbsp cadmium red, mellowed with ¹/₂tbsp burnt umber. Again 360g (12³/₄oz) sand was added to the base coat.

INSTRUCTIONS

Base coat

Pour the emulsion into a container. Add the sand, stirring well. Apply to the prepared surface. Allow to dry (2–3 hours).

Glaze coat

1 Pour the emulsion into the other container. Add the acrylic scumble, yellow ochre, raw sienna, and water (a little at a time) and stir well.
2 Apply to the base coat in random brush strokes (see p. 34). Work over the glaze several times, still allowing some of the base coat to show through. Leave to dry (2–3 hours).

Notes For a hardwearing finish, apply one coat of varnish and allow to dry (2–3 hours).
Exterior use Use textured masonry paint for the base coat (no sand needed) and finish with matt polyurethane varnish.

Paint finishes on wood can be as authentic or fantastic as you wish. Colour is the determining factor. By mixing your own paints, glazes and stains you can, for example, match furnishings and furniture perfectly, creating highly individual schemes. With today's wide choice of colours, the scope for experiment is enormous. Staining, a popular and simple way of treating wood, can look amazing, and it is possible, working with water-based paints, to create softer and paler tones than are now available commercially. Woodwashing is another revelation: this subtle way of adding vibrancy and colour to wood offers many more possibilites when you mix your own colour.

Above: This aged, bleached-wood look is usually achieved by the simple technique of liming. Apply liming wax, allow to harden for 30 minutes and rub off. Alternatively, brush on a pale antiquing glaze, leave to dry for 10 minutes and again rub off.

Conversely, the richness of plain, well-loved wood – whether it be panelling or antique or country furniture – is always appealing, and it is a delight to realize that you can achieve the authentic, aged look seen in period houses simply with the use of paint effects undertaken for very little cost on inexpensive wood surfaces. Junk shops and reclamation yards are ideal hunting grounds for interesting pieces, and wooden architectural features make excellent projects too.

Paint effects can also 'age' new wood quickly. This is important in a period setting, where new wood is often ill at ease. Stairs, handrails, floors and frames can also be aged to add a period feel to any home.

Right: The peeling and cracking surfaces of ageing paint on wood (see p. 128): a good example of an atmospheric effect which works well in traditional interiors. Here subtle shades of green complement the natural brick.

Remember, for authenticity, that the placing and amount of ageing must be determined by the degree of exposure the wood would receive naturally. That said, the effect can be, of course, as subtle or as bold as you like, and there are many simple ways of adding instant patina to a surface. One of the easiest is to rub on a glaze tinted to a deeper tone than the original wood to mimic the natural accumulation of dust and grime over time: you can use dark wood tones in large spaces, but it is wiser to stick to the paler ones in smaller rooms.

Wood finishes are an ideal treatment for kitchens. A new kitchen is always expensive, but using cheaper woods, which can then be aged or have a wood finish applied, can create an expensive, exclusive look at a fraction of the cost. Wood finishes can also transform or totally revitalize an existing kitchen, making it look like new – or old!

The appearance of aged paint on wood is very popular now and, once again, easy to achieve. The effect can be dramatic if you use bright, contemporary colours, but for a simpler, sun-bleached look, liming or applying a pale glaze to wood may be all that is required. For 'authenticity', do not varnish these finishes: they appear with daily wear and tear. Crackle-varnish finishes are more complicated but very beautiful.

Many of these wood finishes can be successfully applied to various surfaces. Study the colour code at the beginning of each entry and check the key on page 41.

Top: Shaker style has influenced this interior. Milk paints were used for an authentic ageing paint on wood effect (see pp. 128 and 134).

Above: Naturally aged wood in a country interior. Study signs of real wear and tear before trying to simulate this look (see p. 104).

AGEING

Wood ages naturally through general wear and tear. Furniture exposed to sunlight fades, and polished wood slowly darkens as it collects dust and grime. It is that sense of time past that gives any well-used and loved piece its appeal, and since the nineteenth century craftsmen have striven to simulate this look on new wood. Virtually any wood can be artificially aged, and there are any number of reasons for wanting to do so. Perhaps you have a new pine bedroom chest that needs to be aged to fit comfortably alongside older pieces. Or maybe a move to a more traditional home has left some of your modern pieces looking out of place. The distressing techniques suggested in my recipe may seem a little drastic, but it is down to you to decide how far to go.

BASIC RECIPE – AGEING PINE

INGREDIENTS

Antiquing glaze ► 500ml PVA adhesive or white glue / 1 litre water / 40g (1²/₅oz) raw sienna powder pigment / 40g (1²/₅oz) raw umber powder pigment (one coat)
Optional protective coat ► 500ml clear matt acrylic varnish (one coat)

EQUIPMENT

Bradawl or 50mm (2in) nail and hammer / craft knife (optional) / container for mixing glaze / 1 x 75mm (3in) household brush / lint-free cotton rags / 1 x 50mm (2in) varnish brush (optional)

This modern pine chest has been aged with a glaze that suggests something of the look of liming. You can still see the original colour – just inside the open drawer. The PVA adhesive solution was coloured with 40g (1²/₅oz) burnt umber and 30g (1oz) white powder pigment. The modern knobs were replaced with others more in keeping with its aged look.

INSTRUCTIONS

Distressing the wood

Use the bradawl (or nail and hammer) to make the small clusters of holes typical of woodworm. You can also, if you like, add occasional scratches, using a craft knife, and small indentations with the hammer.

Antiquing glaze

1 Pour the PVA adhesive (or white glue) into the container. Add the water (a little at a time) and stir well.

2 Add the raw sienna and raw umber and again stir well, making sure that no lumps remain.

3 Brush the glaze onto your prepared surface in random strokes (see p. 34).

4 Make a flat pad of cotton rag and use it to rub the glaze into the surface, paying particular attention to the distressed areas. (This process will also help remove any excess glaze.) Change the rag frequently as it will quickly become clogged with glaze. On small areas the drying time is approx. 1 hour; if you are ageing a large surface, such as a floor, work on an area no larger than 2m² (6ft²) at a time.

Notes Repeat the glaze stage for a greater depth of colour. For a more hardwearing finish apply one or two coats of varnish, allowing 2–3 hours for each coat to dry.

❶ AGEING PINE
Here the basic recipe colourway is applied to a new pine drawer. The resulting dark colour represents the look pine wood might acquire after some years in a hardworking area such as a kitchen.

❷ OCHRE ON ASH
This paler tone is made by colouring the glaze with 60g (2oz) yellow ochre and 20g (³/₄oz) raw umber. The resulting effect works well with old pine. The original wood was ash, which has a greyish tone.

❸ GREY ON LIMED WOOD
Two antiquing glazes are used to create a grey tone on limed wood. The first glaze is tinted with 30g (1oz) white and 20g (³/₄oz) black, while the second one is coloured with 20g (³/₄oz) burnt umber and 10g (¹/₃oz) ultramarine blue.

SPATTER

Spatter is a useful technique which forms the basis of a variety of paint finishes (see, for example, granite and porphyry in Stone finishes), but it is also fun to use the technique alone. It works well on architectural features, such as pillars, moulding and panelling, and on small items of furniture. But avoid the temptation to spatter walls: over a large area those tiny dots can create weird optical effects. Spattering looks easy, but achieving a pleasing, even effect takes practice: follow the advice on p. 36 and practise, practise, practise before you begin. It is also a difficult finish to control – careful masking and protection are essential.

❶ GOLD
The basic recipe: for mouldings.

❷ RED
Base colour: pre-mixed deep red. Spatter colours (all 1tbsp): 1st, raw umber; 2nd, alizarin crimson; 3rd, yellow ochre; 4th, white.

❸ OYSTER
Base colour: 2tbsp neutral grey and 1tbsp burnt umber. Spatter colours: 1st, 1tbsp raw umber; 2nd, 1tbsp neutral grey; 3rd, 1/2tbsp neutral grey and 1/2tbsp titanium white; 4th, 1tbsp titanium white.

❹ BLUE
Base colour: 1tbsp cobalt blue and 2tbsp permanent light blue. Spatter colours: 1st, 1tbsp ultramarine; 2nd, 1tbsp neutral grey; 3rd, 1/2tbsp cobalt blue and 1/2tbsp titanium white; 4th, 1tbsp titanium white.

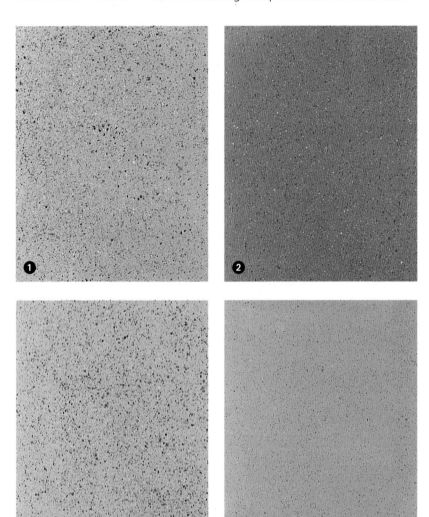

BASIC RECIPE – GOLD IN FOUR COLOURS

INGREDIENTS

Base coat ▶ 500ml white vinyl matt emulsion / 1tbsp venetian red artists' acrylic colour / 1tbsp raw umber artists' acrylic colour / 1/2tbsp yellow ochre artists' acrylic colour

First spatter coat ▶ 1tbsp burnt umber artists' acrylic colour / 1tbsp water

Second spatter coat ▶ 1tbsp raw sienna artists' acrylic colour / 1tbsp water
Third spatter coat ▶ 1tbsp yellow ochre artists' acrylic colour / 1tbsp water
Fourth spatter coat ▶ 1tbsp titanium white artists' acrylic colour / 1tbsp water
Optional protective coat ▶ 500ml clear matt or satin acrylic varnish (one coat)

EQUIPMENT
Container for paint / 1 x 50mm (2in) emulsion brush / dustsheets / masking tape / rag / 4 small pots or jars for glaze / disposable gloves / 4 x 25mm (1in) fitches / 1 x 50mm (2in) varnish brush (optional)

INSTRUCTIONS
Base coat

1 Pour the emulsion into the container. Add the venetian red, raw umber and yellow ochre and stir well.
2 Apply an even coat (see p. 34) to your prepared surface with the 50mm (2in) brush and allow to dry (2–3 hours).

Spatter coats

1 Lay down the dustsheets to protect the surrounding areas and use masking tape to cover any parts of the surface you do not wish to spatter – the spray will go everywhere. (It is wise to remove most of the tackiness on a rag before sticking the tape onto the surface.)
2 Place each of the four acrylic colours into a separate small pot (or jar). Add the water to each and stir well.
3 Put on the gloves and load the first fitch with the darkest glaze. Tap it firmly against another clean, dry fitch held about 15–25cm (6–10in) away from the surface. Your aim is to create a 'mist' of small paint dots of various sizes (see p. 36). It is important to determine the correct loading of paint on the brush before you begin to spatter: consistency is one of the greatest problems with this technique. Work from top to bottom of the surface, concentrating on a wide area to avoid a 'column' effect and taking care not to leave any bald patches.
4 Repeat step 3 with the other spatter coats, using a clean brush for each and applying the darkest glaze first and finishing with the white. You can vary each coat by changing the distance from the wall at which you hold the stationary brush. Allow all coats to dry (2 hours).

Spatter adds individuality to this simple stool. A premixed deep ultramarine blue base coat was used and the spatter colours were: 1st, 1/2tbsp cobalt blue and 1/2tbsp white; 2nd, 1/2tbsp ultramarine blue and 1/2tbsp black; 3rd, 1tbsp yellow ochre; and 4th, 1tbsp titanium white.

Notes Apply one or two coats of matt or satin varnish if a hardwearing finish is required, allowing 2–3 hours for each coat to dry. You can also spatter by loading a toothbrush or similar flat, hard-bristled brush with paint and flicking back the bristles with your fingers, but determine the correct loading of paint on the brush before you begin.

GRAINING

Mastering the art of wood graining might seem almost impossible, but following the principles outlined here will help you to achieve some pleasing results. Whether your aim is authenticity or a fantasy effect, it is a good idea to research the woods you wish to simulate and keep picture references by you as you paint. Remember that using a water-based glaze means you have to work quickly, but the reduced drying time is an advantage. Using some of the modern tools evolved from those of the seventeenth-century craftsmen who first developed the skill, you can produce slightly mechanical wood graining effects in a fraction of the time these recipes demand (see the Notes on p. 111). Handled with sensitivity, such equipment can sometimes produce attractive results (see also p. 138).

BASIC RECIPE – MAHOGANY

INGREDIENTS

Base coats ▶ 1 litre premixed rust brown low-odour eggshell paint
First glaze coat ▶ 50g (1³/₄oz) whiting or chalk powder / 50g (1³/₄oz) vandyke brown powder pigment / 25g (⁹/₁₀oz) raw umber powder pigment / 15g (¹/₂oz) burnt umber powder pigment / 5tbsp water
First sealant coat ▶ 500ml clear satin polyurethane varnish
Second glaze coat ▶ 25g (⁹/₁₀oz) whiting / 25g (⁹/₁₀oz) vandyke brown powder pigment / 15g (¹/₂oz) black powder pigment / 5tbsp water
Second sealant coat ▶ 500ml clear satin polyurethane varnish

EQUIPMENT

5 x 50mm (2in) household brushes / rags / water to dampen the rags / 2 containers for glaze / spalter or mottler / badger softener or 1 x 75mm (3in) soft-bristled emulsion brush / 2 x 25mm (1in) fitches (for mouldings) / dragging brush

Above: A pale mahogany, a variation on the basic recipe. Base coats: 1 litre white eggshell and 50g (1³/₄oz) red oxide powder pigment. Glaze coats: follow basic recipe, adding 10g (¹/₃oz) red oxide for each coat.

Below: Light oak, a variation on the basic recipe. Base coats: 1 litre white eggshell and 2tbsp yellow ochre artists' oil colour. First glaze-colour: 50g (1³/₄oz) yellow ochre and 50g (1³/₄oz) raw sienna. Second glaze-colour: as the first, plus 25g (⁹/₁₀oz) raw umber.

INSTRUCTIONS ALWAYS WORK IN A WELL-VENTILATED AREA

Base coats Stir the eggshell paint well and, using one of the household brushes, apply two even coats (see p. 34) to your prepared surface, allowing 24 hours for each coat to dry.

First glaze coat

1 Soak a rag in water and wring it out thoroughly. Use it to apply a thin film of whiting over the entire surface. You are creating a rougher surface to which the glaze will adhere.

2 Place the vandyke brown, raw umber and burnt umber in one of the containers and add the water (a little at a time), stirring well.

3 Using a second household brush, apply the glaze to the panel in random strokes (see p. 34), excluding mouldings.

4 Take the spalter (or mottler) and drag or draw the glaze downwards in a series of overlapping strokes, trying not to stop midway through a stroke (see p. 37).

5 Using the mottler (or spalter), create the grain effect by working from one corner in overlapping arcs (see p. 37).

6 Tap the badger softener (or 75mm / 3in soft-bristled emulsion brush) lightly over the surface of the glaze, using short, upward strokes (see p. 34). Your aim is to soften the arc effect slightly so that it looks more natural. Clean the brush on a rag often – it must stay fairly dry.

7 Use one of the fitches to apply glaze to any mouldings, working with sweeping horizontal or vertical strokes as the mouldings dictate. Allow to dry (3–4 hours).

First sealant coat Apply one coat of varnish with a third household brush and allow to dry (24 hours).

Second glaze coat

1 Using another damp rag, apply a second thin coat of whiting to the surface. This dulls the first glaze and adds depth of colour to the final effect.

2 Place the vandyke brown and black in the other container. Add the water (a little at a time) and stir well.

3 Using a fourth household brush, apply the glaze to the surface in random strokes, again avoiding any mouldings.

4 Repeat First glaze coat, steps 4 and 5.

5 Tap the dragging brush gently over the surface to create a slight flecking effect on the graining (see p. 36). Clean the bristles on a rag from time to time.

6 If there are any mouldings, repeat First glaze coat, step 7, using the other fitch. Allow to dry (3–4 hours).

Second sealant coat Apply one coat of varnish with a fifth household brush and allow to dry (24 hours).

GRAINING

❶ MAHOGANY
The basic recipe:
(see p. 108).

❷ DARK OAK
The variation:
equally versatile.

❸ PALE GREEN
Wood graining and
the modern palette.
Follow basic recipe.
Base coats: 2tbsp
neutral grey pow-
der pigment and
1 litre white egg-
shell. Glaze-coats
colour-mix: 50g
($1^3/4$oz) viridian
green and 25g
($9/10$oz) white.

❹ DARK GREEN
Follow basic recipe.
Base coats: 2tbsp
viridian green oil
colour and 1 litre
white eggshell.
1st glaze colours:
50g ($1^3/4$oz) bright
green and 50g
($1^3/4$oz) viridian
green; 2nd: 50g
($1^3/4$oz) viridian
green, 25g ($9/10$oz)
bright green and
25g ($9/10$oz) burnt
umber.

VARIATION – DARK OAK

INGREDIENTS

Base coats ► 1 litre premixed bamboo ochre emulsion
First glaze coat ► 150ml acrylic scumble glaze / 25g ($9/10$oz) raw sienna powder pigment / 10g ($1/3$oz) raw umber powder pigment / 5tbsp water
Second glaze coat ► 250ml acrylic scumble glaze / 25g ($9/10$oz) raw sienna powder pigment / 15g ($1/2$oz) burnt umber powder pigment / 5tbsp water
Protective coat ► 500ml clear satin polyurethane varnish

EQUIPMENT

3 x 50mm (2in) emulsion brushes / 3 containers for mixing glaze and for scumble / badger softener or 1 x 75mm (3in) soft-bristled emulsion brush / rags / 2 x 25mm (1in) fitches (for mouldings) / 1 x 25mm (1in) flat artists' brush / 1 x 50mm (2in) household brush

INSTRUCTIONS
Base coat

Stir the emulsion well and apply two good, even coats (see p. 34) to your prepared surface with one of the 50mm (2in) emulsion brushes, working in the direction of the grain and allowing 2–3 hours for each coat to dry.

First glaze coat

1 Place the acrylic scumble in one of the containers. Add the raw sienna, raw umber, and water (a little at a time), stirring well.

2 Using a second 50mm (2in) emulsion brush, apply the glaze to the panel in rough, random strokes (see p. 34), excluding any mouldings.

3 Use the same brush to drag or draw the glaze downwards in a series of overlapping strokes, trying not to stop midway through a stroke (see p. 35).

4 Lightly tap the surface with the badger softener (or soft-bristled emulsion brush) to soften the effect of the dragging (see p. 34). Clean the brush on a rag at regular intervals – it should be fairly dry at all times.

5 Use one of the fitches to apply glaze to any mouldings, working with sweeping horizontal or vertical strokes as the mouldings dictate. Allow to dry (2–3 hours).

Second glaze coat

1 Pour 150ml acrylic scumble into a second container and apply to the surface with a third 50mm (2in) emulsion brush. Leave until it becomes tacky (30 minutes).

2 Place the remaining 100ml acrylic scumble in a third container. Add the raw sienna, burnt umber, and water (a little at a time), stirring well.

3 Using the flat artists' brush, apply this glaze to the tacky surface, excluding any mouldings. Begin by painting an ellipse in the centre of the panel and repeat the shape in a series of ever larger, overlapping, irregular ellipses as you work away from the centre.

4 Soften the grain effect with the badger softener, this time working in gentle, upward strokes and skimming lightly over the surface. Remember to clean the brush regularly.

5 If there are any mouldings, repeat First glaze coat, step 5, using the other fitch. Allow to dry (2–3 hours).

Protective coat

Apply one coat of polyurethane varnish with the household brush and allow to dry (24 hours).

Notes The spalter and mottler mentioned in the basic recipe (see also pp. 29, 30 and 37) are classic wood graining tools, but fan brushes (see p. 29) and simple feathers can create authentic, fine-grained effects. (However, feathers quickly become clogged with paint so you must have a good supply of them.) Rubber combs and rockers (see pp. 29 and 37) will create pronounced and much cruder effects, but they are useful if you are working on a large area, as is the multi-brush pencil grainer (see p. 29).

WATER-BASED CRACKLE

The simulation of the crazing that appears on painted or varnished furniture when the underlying wood expands and contracts as a result of changes in temperature was first undertaken in France as early as the eighteenth century. Today, with the help of proprietary preparations, this ageing technique seems almost magical in its simplicity. One or two coats of a transparent crackle varnish (or craquelure) are applied over a coloured base coat which has been allowed to dry. As the crackle varnish itself dries, it begins to work against the base coat and cracks appear in its surface. Then, when the contrasting top coat is applied and left to dry, the base-coat colour is thrown into relief and the cracks become even more apparent. Tinted glazes can also be rubbed into the surface to enhance and antique the finish. The effect is traditional or contemporary, depending on the colour combination you choose. A natural for wood and plaster – it captures something of the ageing often seen on Italian Renaissance frescos and painted panels – crackle can also translate even the ugliest plastic laminate into a new dimension.

BASIC RECIPE – STONE ON BLUE

INGREDIENTS

Base coat ▶ 500ml premixed sky blue vinyl matt emulsion
Crackle coat ▶ 250ml acrylic crackle varnish (transparent)
Top coat ▶ 500ml premixed stone emulsion
Optional antiquing coat ▶ 250ml pale antiquing patina
Protective coat ▶ 500ml clear satin acrylic varnish (one coat)

EQUIPMENT

2 x 50mm (2in) emulsion brushes / 1 x 25 (1in) household brush / 1 x 50mm (2in) varnish brush / rags (optional)

INSTRUCTIONS
Base coat

Stir the emulsion well and apply one coat to your prepared surface, using one of the emulsion brushes. Allow to dry (2–3 hours). A premixed emulsion reacts much more effectively against the crackle varnish so do not be tempted to mix your own colour.

Crackle coat

Using the household brush, apply one coat of crackle varnish to the entire surface, working horizontally if you want horizontal cracks and vertically if you want vertical ones. As it dries, the varnish begins to crack or craze. The thicker this coat is the fewer and larger the cracks will be; the more it is worked the finer and more numerous. Allow to dry (2 hours).

Above left: The horizontal crazing on this simple MDF box was created by brushing a single coat of water-based crackle varnish in one direction over a base of premixed stone emulsion. The top coat is a premixed deep blue emulsion.

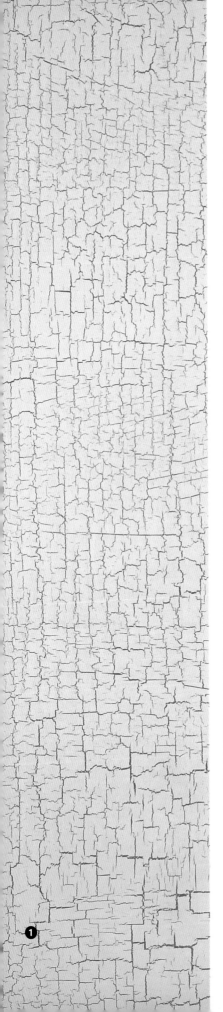

❶ STONE ON BLUE
The basic colour-way: two coats of crackle varnish are applied in opposite directions for an attractive, heavily crazed effect. The final two coats of protective varnish will make this an extremely durable surface.

❷ PEA ON STRAW
Two coats of crackle varnish, again cross brushed, over a base coat of straw-coloured emulsion: the pea green of the top coat was widely used in Victorian times so this scheme would suit a nineteenth-century interior.

❸ SOFT LILAC ON ICECREAM YELLOW
This colourway works well in a modern setting. Here again two coats of cross-brushed crackle varnish are used.

❹ DEEP RED ON STONE
For a colour combination popular in the Victorian era: a stone emulsion base coat under a deep red top coat. Only one coat of crackle was applied in vertical strokes.

❺ WARM GREY ON BRICK
The deep red base under warm grey is typical of the Georgian period, and the two coats of crackle varnish are cross brushed and well worked to create fine crazing.

WATER-BASED CRACKLE

Top coat   Stir the emulsion well, brush an even coat (see p. 34) onto the crazed surface using the other emulsion brush, and leave to dry (2–3 hours). As the top coat dries, the cracks will become apparent once more, revealing the blue of the base coat. (You can speed the drying process with a hairdryer.)

Protective coat   Using the varnish brush, apply one coat of varnish and allow to dry (2–3 hours). Repeat if a particularly hardwearing finish is required.

Notes If you want an even more pronounced effect, repeat the crackle stage before applying the top coat, brushing the varnish on in the opposite direction. For a more antique finish, use a rag to rub in a layer of antiquing patina after the top coat has dried and leave to dry (1 hour) before applying the protective coat.

The palest green water-based crackle on a panelled wall could work wonderfully well in a period setting. This charming setting suggests the lightness of the rococo period.

114

OIL-BASED CRACKLE

Oil-based crackle produces an effect of greater age than its water-based counterpart (see p. 112) and cracks tend to be more widely spaced and varied. Here two layers of transparent crackle varnish are standard, and they work against each other while drying. A tinted glaze brushed on and rubbed off to remain only in the cracks completes the effect. The look can be subtle or bold, depending on the colour contrast. Oil-based crackle varnish is an unpredictable material. Experience has taught me three things: follow the manufacturer's instructions, use premixed paint for the base coat, and work in an evenly heated, dry area. It is also best confined to small, flat surfaces. But do not be put off. Crackle is a remarkable finish that can produce wonderful results.

BASIC RECIPE – RED ON BLACK

INGREDIENTS

Base coat ► 500ml premixed black gloss paint
Crackle coats ► 1 litre premixed oil-based crackle varnish (transparent)
Top coat ► 2tbsp cadmium red artists' oil colour / 1tbsp premixed oil-based scumble glaze / 1tbsp white spirit
Optional protective coats ► 1 litre clear satin or gloss polyurethane varnish

EQUIPMENT

2–3 x 50mm (2in) household brushes / 1 x 25mm (1in) varnish brush / container for mixing glaze / rags

INSTRUCTIONS

Base coat

ALWAYS WORK IN A WELL-VENTILATED AREA

Stir the gloss paint thoroughly and use one of the household brushes to apply two even coats (see p. 34) to your prepared surface, allowing 24 hours for each coat to dry.

Crackle coats

1 Apply an even coat of crackle varnish to the entire surface, using the varnish brush, and leave to become tacky (approx. 30 minutes).
2 Brush on a second coat and allow both coats to dry completely (1 hour). As the second coat dries, it pulls against the first, creating fine cracks in the surface of the varnish.

Two variations on the basic recipe: (left) a dark green gloss base coat and a top coat tinted with 2tbsp jaune brillant; (right) a deep red gloss base coat and a top-coat colour-mix of 1tbsp titanium white, 1/2tbsp cadmium red and 1/2tbsp jaune brillant.

❶ RED ON BLACK
The classic colour-
way of the basic
recipe: a striking
combination which
works well with
Chinese antiques.

❷ BLUE ON OCHRE
This modern look
can find a place in
a traditional home.
A deep antique yel-
low is used for the
gloss base coat,
and the top coat
is coloured with
2$\frac{1}{2}$tbsp cobalt
blue and $\frac{1}{2}$tbsp
titanium white.

**❸ RED ON
ANTIQUE YELLOW**
An authentic look:
cracks in the stone
gloss base coat are
revealed with a top-
coat colour-mix of
1tbsp yellow ochre,
$\frac{1}{2}$tbsp red oxide
and $\frac{1}{2}$tbsp raw
umber.

**❹ PALE GREY
ON BURGUNDY**
Another bold
colourway in the
oriental style.
The crazing over
the burgundy gloss
base coat is tinted
with a top coat
coloured with
1tbsp neutral grey
and 1tbsp titanium
white.

Top coat

1 Place the cadmium red in the container. Add the oil-based scumble and white spirit and stir well.

2 Apply an even coat to the entire surface, using a second household brush.

3 Wipe most of the glaze off with clean rags – when you have finished, red glaze should remain only in the cracks. It is important to keep changing rags or you will begin recoating the surface with glaze. Allow to dry (24 hours).

Notes For a more hardwearing finish, apply two coats of varnish with a third household brush, allowing 24 hours for each coat to dry.

Staining is an easy way of transforming and protecting wood. Oil-based or water-based colours can be used, and which you choose depends on the effect you want to create. The oil-based method – adding colour to melted wax – is the traditional approach, putting the whole oil-colour palette at your disposal. It is also the most effective: the wax dries to a tough finish and the colour does not fade easily. But oil-colour pigments are strong. Used with care, staining with water-based colours can create a softer look. Varnishing is essential on this less durable finish.

BASIC RECIPE – OIL-BASED DEEP RED

INGREDIENTS	1 x 50g (1³/₄oz) beeswax pellets / 2tbsp cadmium red artists' oil colour / 1tbsp venetian red artists' oil colour / ¹/₂tbsp raw umber artists' oil colour
EQUIPMENT	Double boiler or *bain-marie* / old wooden spoon / lint-free cloths / 1 x 50mm (2in) household brush (optional) / shoe-polish brush (optional)
INSTRUCTIONS	**1** Using the double boiler (or *bain-marie*), place the beeswax pellets in the upper container and gently melt them down to a smooth liquid, stirring from time to time with the spoon. **2** Add the cadmium red, venetian red and raw umber and mix well. Allow to dry to a soft paste (approx. 10 minutes). **3** Make a pad with lint-free cloth and spread the wax evenly over your prepared surface, rubbing it in carefully. (You can

❶ DEEP RED
The basic colour-way: this rich tone is typical of oil-based staining.

❷ ULTRAMARINE
Again the colour is strong and deep: 3tbsp ultramarine blue in the stain.

❸ DEEP YELLOW
Fun to use, it might show dark markings so is best used in small sections of a floor pattern. The colour-mix is 2¹/₂tbsp cadmium yellow and ¹/₂tbsp yellow ochre.

❹ UMBER
A practical colour and a natural look: 2tbsp burnt umber and 1tbsp raw sienna make up the tint.

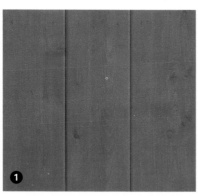

also use a household brush to apply the wax.) When staining large areas, it is wise to work on sections no larger than 1m² (3ft²) at a time. Allow to dry (2 hours).

4 Polish with a clean rag (or shoe-polish brush) – the wax stain creates a rich, transparent gloss finish.

Exterior use Finish with two coats of satin polyurethane varnish, allowing 24 hours for each coat to dry.

WATER-BASED STAINING

You can make water-based stains quite easily by dissolving powder colour in water. Fabric or spirit dyes or powder pigments are all effective, and a wide range of colours is available. Some create extremely strong colours so experiment on a spare piece of wood before committing yourself to any scheme. See the caption opposite for how to mix powder pigments. For fabric or spirit dyes, start by mixing 1tsp of colour with 500ml of water and add water or colour until you have the shade you want. It is important to apply all these stains evenly to prevent them from drying patchily. Seal with matt, satin or gloss acrylic varnish for a durable finish.

STAINING A PATTERNED FLOOR

Patterned floors are an attractive way of improving old floor boards in bad condition or cheap wooden floor coverings – anything, in fact, that would not reward the close scrutiny stripped and sealed floors attract. Choose a geometric design, and keep the pattern large and simple or the job will take forever. Measure the floor area and draw a scale plan on graph paper. Tape a piece of tracing paper over the floor plan and sketch your design onto it, making

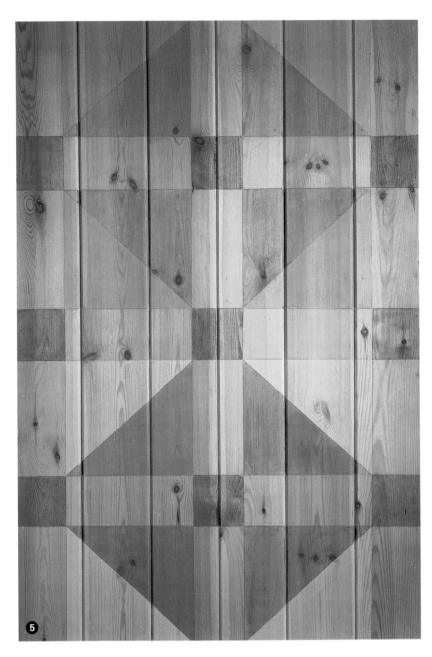

❺ WATER-BASED STAINING
This simple floor design was undertaken according to the method outlined opposite. All the colours were powder pigment, mixed to a ratio of one part pigment, two parts water. Quantities will vary according to the area you wish to cover. For this area (1.25 x 1.5m/4 x 5ft), the colours and quantities used were as follows.

Green triangles: 25g (⁹/₁₀oz) moss green and 2tbsp water. Blue triangles: 25g (⁹/₁₀oz) cobalt blue and 2tbsp water. Dark pink triangles: 12.5g (²/₅oz) rose madder pink, 12.5g (²/₅oz) white and 2tbsp water. Pale pink triangles: 12.5g (²/₅oz) yellow ochre, 12.5g (²/₅oz) white and 2tbsp water. Cross bands: 25g (⁹/₁₀oz) yellow ochre and 2tbsp water. Squares: 12.5g (²/₅oz) black, 12.5g (²/₅oz) white and 2tbsp water.

adjustments to fit the dimensions of the floor. This is also the time to decide how to use the colours you have chosen. Try out your ideas in a series of rough colour sketches, using markers or coloured pencils. When you have made your choice, add the colours to your master tracing, filling the areas in carefully. With pattern and colour decided, use a metre/yard stick and pencil to transfer the pattern to the prepared surface. Following either method described, work with one colour at a time, using masking tape to protect areas that are not to be painted. Allow each colour to dry completely before remasking and applying another.

RUBBING OFF ON WOOD

I have developed this technique to colour and age wood simultaneously in a subtle and stylish way. It is an immensely satisfying method of giving old wood a new lease of life and an equally effective route to creating furniture that blends with your decor. Searching junk shops for old pieces to transform is fun – simple, uncluttered lines are often the most successful. The effect is soft, as some of the wood's colour remains visible, and the detail and graining are still apparent, but dark varnish works against it so have wood stripped if necessary before sealing it. If you decide to work with a new or immaculate piece, you can opt to age it first, and, of course, there is no need to limit yourself to one colour. You could choose one for the legs and back of a chair and another for the seat. Seal the entire surface and use masking tape (removing most of the tackiness on a cloth) to protect areas you do not want to colour with your first glaze. Then apply and rub off as in the recipe; remask and follow the same process for your second colour.

BASIC RECIPE – MOSS GREEN ON BLOND WOOD

INGREDIENTS

Sealant coat ▶ 1 x 500ml white polish
Rubbed-off glaze ▶ 500ml white vinyl matt emulsion / 2tbsp acrylic scumble glaze (transparent) / 1tbsp hooker's green artists' acrylic colour / 1/2tbsp pale olive green artists' acrylic colour / 1/2tbsp yellow ochre artists' acrylic colour / 1tbsp water (one coat)
Optional protective coat ▶ 500ml clear matt or satin acrylic varnish

EQUIPMENT

Bradawl or 50mm (2in) nail and hammer (optional) / craft knife (optional) / lint-free cloths / medium-grade sandpaper / container for mixing glaze / 1 x 50mm (2in) household brush / 1 x 50mm (2in) varnish brush (optional)

INSTRUCTIONS
Ageing (optional)

Use the bradawl (or 50mm/2in nail and hammer) to make the small clusters of holes typical of woodworm in your pre-pared surface. You can also add occasional scratches, using a craft knife, and small indentations with a hammer.

Sealant coat

1 Form a pad, using lint-free cloth, and apply a thin, even coat of white polish. Allow to dry (1 hour) and buff up with a clean cloth.
2 Using the sandpaper, rub lightly over the entire surface. Your aim is to create a slightly rougher surface to which the glaze coat will adhere, but it is important that you do not take off too much of the polish.

Opposite and above: These chairs were stripped and left to dry for 7 days before work began. Colours as follows. Green: basic recipe. Lilac: 1 1/2tbsp pale violet and 1/2tbsp titanium white. Blue: 1 1/2tbsp ultra-marine and 1/2tbsp burnt umber. Sand: 1 1/2tbsp yellow ochre and 1/2tbsp raw umber.

❶ MOSS GREEN ON BLOND WOOD The colours of the basic recipe give a rich tone for a country home. A durable, hardwearing finish, it would do especially well in the kitchen. In all four examples rubbing off in the direction of the grain has produced an effect almost like dragging.

❷ RICH UMBER A versatile colourway that brings a natural, deep tone to the wood: 2tbsp raw umber colour the glaze mix.

❸ VIOLET This contemporary look is created by tinting the glaze with 2tbsp brilliant purple.

❹ TURQUOISE Another bright, modern look, its seaside tones would be fun in a bathroom. The glaze is coloured with 1¹/₂tbsp turquoise blue and ¹/₂tbsp cobalt blue.

Rubbed-off glaze

1 Pour the emulsion into the container. Add the acrylic scumble, hooker's and pale olive greens, yellow ochre, and water (a little at a time), stirring well.

2 Apply the glaze thickly onto the entire surface with the household brush and leave until it becomes tacky (approx. 5 minutes).

3 Using another cloth, wipe most of the glaze off – your aim is to leave a fine haze of colour on the flat surfaces and a build-up of glaze in any detail. Allow to dry (2 hours).

Notes Repeat the Rubbing off stage if you want a greater depth of colour. For a more hardwearing finish, apply a coat of varnish and allow to dry (2–3 hours).

Exterior use Finish with two coats of satin polyurethane varnish, allowing 24 hours for each coat to dry.

Opposite: Here the panelling in a period interior has been rubbed off with a pale colour to give the appearance of limewash. An interesting approach, it gives a traditional, aged effect that complements the antique chair.

WOODWASHING

This simple way to colour wood creates a pale, washed effect. It is ideal for kitchens and for pieces of furniture that you wish to fit into a new scheme or setting. Like the previous finish but even easier to handle, the look is soft, with the graining and detail of the wood still visible. It is also an ideal way to improve the cheaper soft woods, making them an attractive option for the budget conscious. Premixed wood washes are now available but the colour range is limited and mixing your own is cheaper. Varnish surfaces you plan to use in kitchen and bathroom.

❶ DEEP BLUE
The basic recipe: this subtle look, showing plenty of the wood's graining through the glaze, would work well in a kitchen or bathroom.

❷ DUSKY PINK
Another soft colourway with the beauty of the wood still apparent: 1tbsp alizarin crimson, 1tbsp titanium white, 1/2tbsp raw sienna and 1/2tbsp lilac make the delicate tones.

❸ PALE GREEN
A subtle colour, versatile in kitchens and conservatories, it was created by colouring the wash with 2tbsp sap green, 1tbsp raw sienna and 1/2tbsp titanium white.

❹ RAW SIENNA
A versatile colour to enhance most new woods: the colour-mix is 2tbsp raw sienna and 1tbsp raw umber.

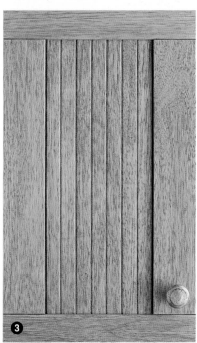

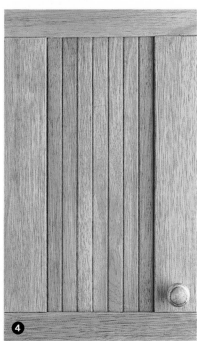

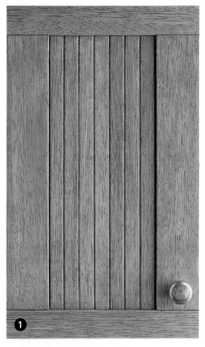

BASIC RECIPE – DEEP BLUE

INGREDIENTS

500ml white vinyl matt emulsion / 2tbsp ultramarine artists' acrylic colour / 1tbsp cobalt blue artists' acrylic colour / ¹/₂tbsp burnt umber artists' acrylic colour / 150–200ml water

Optional protective coat ▶ 500ml clear matt or satin acrylic varnish (one coat)

EQUIPMENT

Container for mixing wash coat / 1 x 75mm (3in) emulsion brush / lint-free cloth / 1 x 50mm (2in) varnish brush (optional)

INSTRUCTIONS

1 Pour the emulsion into the container. Add the ultramarine, cobalt blue, burnt umber, and water (a little at a time), stirring continuously – you are aiming for a milky consistency.
2 Using the emulsion brush, apply the wash to the wood, working always in the direction of the grain – you should be able to see it through the thin wash. Allow to dry a little (15–20 minutes).
3 Make a pad with a lint-free cloth and wipe the surface to reveal further grain and texture. Leave to dry (1 hour).

Above: Door and skirting board have been woodwashed in a lovely blue. This is an ideal finish to complement the stained-plaster look of the walls.

Notes If you want a hardwearing finish, seal with one or two coats of varnish, allowing 2–3 hours for each coat to dry.

Right: The cool, pale blue of this kitchen sideboard unit was mixed to match a well-loved Aga and then subtly distressed (perhaps with wirewool). Finally a layer of liming wax was applied (see caption, p. 102).

Right: Blue adds an interesting note here too, in a fine example of ageing paint on wood (see p. 128). An indigo tone has been painted on the frame of this cupboard: an imaginative addition which lifts an already charming piece, decorated with aged ochre tones.

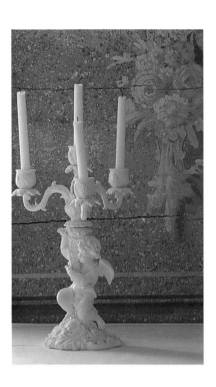

Right: Spatter in two tones of blue (see p. 106) forms the backdrop for accomplished hand painting on a dramatic wall panel. Note the clever use of the same colours in the simple border at the base.

Left: Aged paint on wood again, and this time the inspiration is ethnic. See how the much-painted shelves have acquired a dull, powdery texture. Whiting (50g/1³/₄oz) added to the glaze and rubbed back will re-create this simple effect.

AGEING PAINT

I devised this effective technique to give furniture and fittings the appearance of many layers of paint slowly peeling off after decades of wear and tear. The art of simulating ageing paint, like crackle (see pp. 112-16), dates back to eighteenth-century France, and it is still an excellent way to make cheaper, new wood look as though it has been in your home for years. The finish can have a period look, through the use of dark reds and greens, or a more contemporary one, with bright, contrasting tones; and peeling can be subtle or emphatic, depending on the degree of ageing. To create an authentic look, study genuine old pieces before you begin and discover where natural ageing occurs.

BASIC RECIPE – DEEP YELLOW ON BURNT UMBER

INGREDIENTS
Wax coat ▶ 1 x 250ml tin furniture wax (clear) or beeswax
Wash coat ▶ 2tbsp burnt umber artists' acrylic colour / 1tbsp water
Emulsion coat ▶ 500ml white vinyl matt emulsion / 2tbsp cadmium yellow artists' acrylic colour / 1tbsp bronze ochre artists' acrylic colour ¹/₂tbsp venetian red artists' acrylic colour
Glaze coat ▶ 500ml white vinyl matt emulsion / 1tbsp cadmium yellow artists' acrylic colour / ¹/₂tbsp bronze ochre artists' acrylic colour / 4tbsp water
Optional protective coat ▶ 250ml furniture polish (clear) or 500ml clear satin acrylic varnish

EQUIPMENT
1 x 25mm (1in) household brush / pencil / paper (for sketch plan) / 3 containers for mixing wash, emulsion and glaze / 1 x 25mm (1in) emulsion brush / 2 x 50mm (2in) emulsion brushes / scraper or spatula / rags / medium-grade sandpaper / 1 x 50mm (2in) varnish brush (optional)

INSTRUCTIONS
Wax coat
Using the household brush, dab wax onto those areas of the prepared wooden surface you wish to reveal in the finished effect. This is essentially a resist technique – paint will not adhere permanently to the areas you wax – so you need to visualize what you want to achieve and draw a sketch of it as a reminder when you begin to distress the paint later. Vary the length, shape and spacing of the waxed areas as much as possible. It is best to apply the wax evenly in a series of lines rather than with random strokes. Leave to dry (24 hours).

Wash coat
1 Place the burnt umber in one of the containers and add the water (a little at a time), stirring well.
2 Use the 25mm (1in) emulsion brush to apply the wash to the wood in the direction of the grain. Allow to dry (1 hour).

Emulsion coat
1 Pour the emulsion into a second container. Add the cadmium yellow, bronze ochre and venetian red and stir well.

Opposite: This new occasional table was aged using a shortened version of the ageing paint technique. The bright yellow was created by using 3tbsp cadmium yellow in the wash, the emulsion coat was omitted, and the glaze was coloured with 2tbsp bright green.

AGEING PAINT

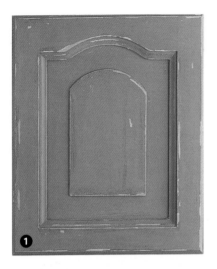

❶ DEEP YELLOW ON BURNT UMBER
The basic recipe: this natural mix is typical of French country furniture and would be good in a kitchen, where it makes a hard-wearing finish.

❷ BURGUNDY ON CORAL
There is a country feel to this rich colourway too, another variation on the basic recipe. Here a wash coat is not used. The emulsion coat is tinted with 2tbsp cadmium red, 1/2tbsp titanium white and 1/2tbsp raw sienna. The glaze-coat mix uses 2tbsp raw sienna and 1tbsp red oxide.

❸ PALE BLUE ON ULTRAMARINE
Again the wash coat is omitted. The emulsion coat is coloured with 3tbsp ultramarine blue, and the glaze with 1tbsp cobalt blue, 1tbsp light ultramarine blue and 1tbsp titanium white.

❹ PURPLE ON STONE
This contemporary version tints the wash coat with 50g (1³/₄oz) yellow ochre powder pigment. The other coats revert to acrylic colour: for the emulsion, 3tbsp yellow ochre; for the glaze 2tbsp brilliant purple and 1tbsp cobalt blue.

2 Using one of the 50mm (2in) emulsion brushes, apply an even coat of paint to the surface in the direction of the grain. Allow to dry (2–3 hours).

Glaze coat

1 Pour the emulsion into a third container. Add the cadmium yellow, bronze ochre, and water (gradually), stirring well.
2 Apply an even coat in the direction of the grain, using the other 50mm (2in) emulsion brush. Allow to dry a little (30–40 minutes).

Distressing the paint

1 Referring to your sketch plan, use the scraper (or spatula) and rags to remove as many layers of paint as you can in the waxed areas.
2 Smooth the rough edges of the paint with sandpaper.

Notes If you want a more hardwearing finish, seal the surface with a layer of furniture polish or with a coat of varnish, which will take 2–3 hours to dry.

SCANDINAVIAN

This door has been painted in tones typical of the Scandinavian palette, using an ageing paint technique (see p. 128), and the wall painting is a characteristic floral design.

In recent years the Scandinavian colour palette has become increasingly popular. It is a look that derives largely from nature. The misty, cool blues and greens of those northern landscapes predominate, spiked with a variety of earth tones in the highly decorated detailing of plants and flowers. It was in the long winter months, when the elements prevented work on the land, that peasant men and women spent many hours carving and painting the cupboards, dressers and chests that are now so much admired. A characteristic simplicity of form and airy lightness of effect make this an ideal look for kitchens and bathrooms.

In this recipe I have devised a simple, undecorated, aged finish which works well with the Scandinavian colour palette. As a broken-colour technique – that is, as a glaze applied on a contrasting flat base coat and then rubbed back – it has authenticity, as well as plenty of texture and body. It is ideal for furniture that receives heavy wear and, because it uses water-based products, is easy to apply to most wooden surfaces. This is a charming way of decorating second-hand furniture and rejuvenating old kitchen cupboards.

BASIC RECIPE – BLUE-GREY ON IVY GREEN

INGREDIENTS

Emulsion coat ▶ 500ml white vinyl matt emulsion / 3tbsp hooker's green artists' acrylic colour / 2tbsp pale olive green artists' acrylic colour
Glaze coat ▶ 500ml white vinyl matt emulsion / 3tbsp monestial blue artists' acrylic colour / 1tbsp cobalt blue artists' acrylic colour / 1tbsp paynes grey artists' acrylic colour / 2tbsp water (one coat)
Optional protective coat ▶ 500ml clear satin acrylic varnish

EQUIPMENT

2 x 50mm (2in) emulsion brushes / 2 containers for mixing paint / rags / 1 x 50mm (2in) varnish brush (optional)

SCANDINAVIAN

INSTRUCTIONS

Emulsion coat

1 Pour the emulsion into one of the containers. Add the hooker's and pale olive greens and stir well.

2 Apply to your prepared surface, working in the direction of the grain, and allow to dry (2–3 hours).

Glaze coat

1 Pour the emulsion into the other container. Add the monestial blue, cobalt blue, paynes grey, and water (a little at a time), stirring well

2 Apply to the entire surface in the direction of the grain.

3 When this coat is set but not dry (approx. 30 minutes), wipe off gently with a rag, working again in the direction of the grain to reveal some of the emulsion coat. Allow to dry (2–3 hours).

Notes For a deeper tone, repeat the glaze coat or leave the water out of that stage. If you decide to use no water, the glaze will dry more quickly so do not wait for it to set before

❶ BLUE-GREY ON IVY GREEN
The classic tones and an ideal base for decoration: the glaze coat was left to set for approx. 10 minutes.

❷ GREEN ON STONE
This is made by colouring the emulsion coat with 2tbsp yellow ochre, and the glaze with 3tbsp forest green and 1tbsp monestial green.

❸ GREY ON PALE BLUE
The emulsion coat is tinted with 3tbsp cobalt blue, and the glaze with 3tbsp neutral grey and 2tbsp burnt umber.

❹ CORAL ON UMBER
A modern alternative: colour the emulsion coat with 4tbsp burnt umber, the glaze with 2tbsp raw sienna.

wiping off. If you want a more hardwearing finish, apply one coat of varnish.

Exterior use It is best to follow Scandinavian custom and use wood staining for a tough exterior surface. Follow the basic recipe for oil-based wax staining given on p. 117, substituting artists' oil colours which capture the Scandinavian colour palette (the acrylic colours given here are also available as oil colours). For exterior woodwork, such as window frames and shutters, the same oil-based stains can be used, but remember to finish with one coat of satin polyurethane varnish for extra durability and allow to dry for 24 hours.

The trompe l'oeil *windows contribute to this unusually flamboyant Scandinavian interior. Much more traditional in feel are the handsome panelling and beautifully decorated chair backs.*

SHAKER

The Shaker look seems to speak to many people today. Perhaps it is the simplicity and sheer coherence of the Shaker way of life that appeals. Every aspect of Shaker life was organized and this is reflected in their simple architecture, home decoration and furnishing.

They painted the exteriors of their work buildings in tans and yellows; more expensive white paint was restricted to meeting houses. Their homes were often painted cream, with dark brown, bottle green or deep red woodwork inside. The believers liked bold, solid colours and, although their furnishings were characteristically free of ornamentation, the shapes and colours are extremely attractive.

This deep brown panelling is typical of Shaker colouring. Their unpainted woods were often maple and pine.

In their frugal, self-supporting communities paint was often hard to come by and had to be made from available materials. Whole milk was the usual medium, mixed with costly powder pigments and a little lime,

and the resulting milk (or casein) paints were cheap, durable and easy to apply, drying to a flat, smooth finish with a depth of colour seldom found in synthetic paints. Milk paints can still be bought today, in a wide range of Shaker colours, although now they are sold either premixed with buttermilk or skimmed-milk powders or simply as pigment with instructions for mixing. They are certainly the best way of creating the authentic colours of a Shaker home: I recommend that you use them for this recipe, which depends for its aged effect on an extremely simple resist technique.

BASIC RECIPE – DEEP COLONIAL RED ON YELLOW OCHRE

INGREDIENTS	Base coat ▶ 500ml yellow ochre milk (casein) paint (one coat)
	Wax coat ▶ 500ml beeswax or furniture wax (clear)
	Top coat ▶ 500ml deep red milk (casein) paint
	Optional protective coats ▶ 1 litre clear satin polyurethane varnish
EQUIPMENT	2–3 x 50mm (2in) household brushes / 1 x 25mm (1in) household brush / wirewool / disposable gloves
INSTRUCTIONS	ALWAYS WORK IN A WELL-VENTILATED AREA
Base coat	Stir the yellow ochre milk (casein) paint thoroughly. Using one of the 50mm (2in) household brushes, apply an even coat (see p. 34) to your prepared surface and allow to dry

1 DEEP COLONIAL RED ON OCHRE
The basic recipe: deep tones and density of colour are common on Shaker woodwork. The pale base gives a wonderfully aged effect.

2 ANTIQUE YELLOW ON SOLDIER BLUE
Another popular colourway: the main area of wear is the door knob, but the ageing can be more pronounced if you wish.

3 OCHRE ON DEEP RED
This reverses the colours of the basic recipe for a less imposing effect.

4 SOLDIER BLUE ON OCHRE
A lovely colour-mix and typical of the Shakers' pure tones, this would be good in a kitchen or in a bathroom.

(24 hours). Milk paints create such a flat, smooth finish that you often do not need to add a second coat.

Wax coat Brush a liberal coat of the beeswax onto the areas you wish to distress, using the 25mm (1in) household brush. (The top coat will not adhere permanently wherever there is a wax coating.) Allow to dry (1 hour).

Top coat **1** Stir the deep red milk paint thoroughly and apply a good, even coat with a second 50mm (2in) household brush. Allow to dry (24 hours).
2 Put on the gloves and rub the wirewool gently over the surface, concentrating on the areas where you applied the wax, until you reveal the ochre paint beneath.

Notes For a more hardwearing finish, apply two coats of varnish, using a third 50mm (2in) household brush and allowing 24 hours for each coat to dry.

These trugs were all painted with water-based materials. This gives more scope for colour variation, but do check picture references to maintain the correct feel. Almost all the colours described here are artists' acrylics and were added to 500ml vinyl silk emulsion.

The stone base coat for the brown and dusky pink trugs was coloured with 2tbsp yellow ochre. The brown top-coat tint was 3tbsp raw umber, 1tbsp yellow ochre and 1tbsp burnt umber. The dusky pink was made by mixing 2tbsp cadmium red, 1tbsp raw umber and 1/4tbsp cobalt blue.

The green was created with 3tbsp sap green and 1tbsp raw umber, and applied to the dusky pink described above. The blue was a premixed vinyl silk emulsion and was applied to a base coat coloured with 2tbsp cobalt blue.

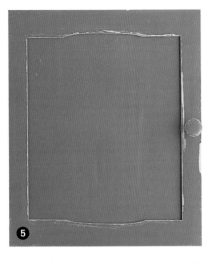

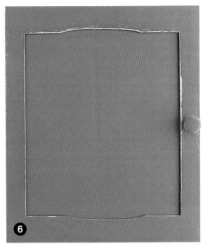

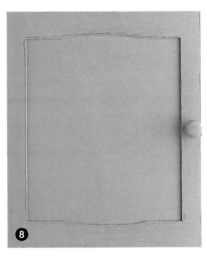

❺ SEA GREEN ON WHITE
The green is made by adding 3tbsp chromium green and 1tbsp cobalt blue to 500ml white vinyl silk emulsion: a clean colourway with a different feel but still in the Shaker tradition.

❻ TERRACOTTA ON GREY
This rich combination would make a good choice for a kitchen or bathroom. The terracotta is a premixed vinyl silk emulsion, but the base coat adds 2tbsp neutral grey to 500ml white vinyl silk emulsion.

❼ CREAM ON PALE BLUE
A light colour-mix but again typical of Shaker taste: the base coat is made by adding 2tbsp cobalt blue to 500ml white vinyl silk emulsion; the cream by adding 2tbsp yellow ochre to 500ml white vinyl silk emulsion.

❽ PALE BLUE ON TERRACOTTA
Another lively alternative: the base coat is the premixed terracotta used in sample 6, and the top coat adds 3tbsp cobalt blue to 500ml white vinyl silk emulsion.

WATER-BASED SHAKER

Milk (casein) paints take a long time to dry so you may prefer to use water-based vinyl silk emulsion paints instead. These are now available premixed in the deep colours of the Shaker palette, and may be more appealing if you are decorating a small, dark room which could appear a little claustrophobic with surfaces given the dense, flat look characteristic of milk paints. Because of their less toxic qualities, emulsion paints are also the better option for a child's room.

Follow the quantities given in the basic recipe, using premixed paints or colouring 500ml vinyl silk emulsion with artists' acrylic colours as required. You may need two top coats for a finish to equal that of milk paint. Allow 2–3 hours for each coat to dry. Use the beeswax and wirewool as indicated and finally seal with two coats of clear satin acrylic varnish, using a 50mm (2in) varnish brush and allowing 2–3 hours for each coat to dry.

COMBING

Combing evolved from wood graining techniques but has a more formal, non-realistic effect. It has become a popular finish for decorating furniture, but is not advisable for large areas of panelling as it is not easy to keep a steady hand for long. You can combine bold, bright colours, but the most stunning combing is almost always seen on a white or pale base, although working with paler glazes on dark base coats can be effective too. The recipe uses oil-based products because the glaze will remain workable for longer and mistakes can usually be rectified. Rubber combs are readily available (see p. 29) but you can easily make your own from cardboard or a plastic container lid. Working on a horizontal surface is best; if this is not possible, work from a top corner. If you are right-handed, work from the left side; if left-handed, from the right. Using combs of different sizes and working in different directions, you can create many looks, including moiré, crisscross and basket weave. Make up your own for an individual effect.

BASIC RECIPE – BURNT UMBER ON TERRACOTTA

INGREDIENTS

Base coat ▶ 500ml white low-odour eggshell paint / 1^1/2tbsp yellow ochre artists' oil colour / ^{1}/2tbsp venetian red artists' acrylic colour / ^{1}/4tbsp raw umber artists' acrylic colour

Glaze coat ▶ 500ml premixed oil-based scumble glaze (transparent) / 3tbsp burnt umber artists' oil colour / 1tbsp raw umber artists' oil colour / 200ml white spirit

Protective coat ▶ 500ml oil-based dead flat varnish

EQUIPMENT

2 containers for mixing paint and glaze / 3 x 50mm (2in) household brushes / 1 stippling brush or large flat brush / disposable gloves / comb / rags

INSTRUCTIONS

ALWAYS WORK IN A WELL-VENTILATED AREA

Base coat

1 Pour the eggshell paint into one of the containers. Add the yellow ochre, venetian red and raw umber and stir well.

2 Apply evenly to the prepared surface (see p. 34), using one of the household brushes, and allow to dry (24 hours).

Glaze coat

1 Pour the oil-based scumble into the other container. Add the burnt umber, raw umber, and white spirit (a little at a time), stirring well.

2 Apply an even coat of glaze to the surface, using a second household brush.

3 Using the stippling (or flat) brush and light, tapping strokes, eradicate the brush marks (see p. 35).

4 Put on the gloves and hold the comb firmly with its teeth at right angles to the surface while keeping your arm outstretched and as straight as possible. Drag or draw the glaze downwards from top to bottom of the surface, working

across it in a series of strokes (see p. 37). Wipe the comb clean on a rag after each stroke. Try not to overlap strokes or stop midway through one. Double-stroking a mistake never works because you take off more colour, making the effect uneven – wipe the glaze off with a rag soaked in white spirit, brush more on and begin again. Allow to dry (24 hours).

Protective coat   Using a third household brush, apply an even coat of varnish and allow to dry (24 hours).

❶ BURNT UMBER ON TERRACOTTA
The basic recipe: combing is a hard-wearing effect and ideal for all kinds of hardworking furniture. It looks good in a period interior.

❷ YELLOW ON WHITE
This lovely yellow is made with 3tbsp cadmium yellow. The base coat is a simple white eggshell.

❸ DEEP GREEN ON PALE GREEN
The pale base uses 1¹/₂tbsp oxide of chromium. The glaze is coloured with 2tbsp oxide of chromium and ¹/₂tbsp viridian green.

❹ BLUE ON WHITE
Another glaze applied over white eggshell: the blue was made with 2tbsp cobalt blue.

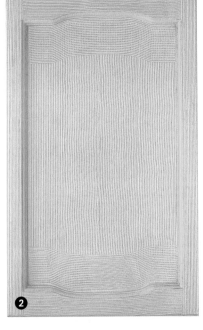

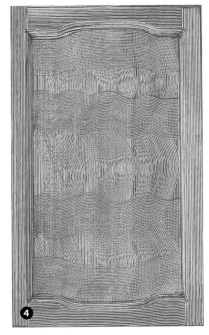

STONE FINISHES

Above: Kitchen
units decorated
with a sandstone
effect similar to
my basic recipe
(see p. 148): these
soft, sponged
tones gently con-
tradict the plain,
functional lines
of the room.

Right: The granite
finish (see p. 152)
on this urn-like
lamp base is
raised well above
the funereal with
unexpected
bands of subtly
aged gilding (see
p. 180). The effect
is both classical
and traditional.

Stone effects are among those called bravura finishes. They are not so much finishes in their own right as tools of the illusionist, designed to fool the beholder into believing that they are genuine. The standard advice is use the bravura finishes only where you would use the real thing, but frankly with a little imagination they can look wonderful in some of the strangest situations, creating effects that range from sheer fantasy to subtle deception.

Many stone finishes, and marble most especially, can be used to create an illusion of boldness and grandeur. Even the smallest space can look opulent given a marble finish; bathrooms are ideal: *faux* panelling, cupboards and even the outside of the bath itself are fun to try. But a larger old house carelessly modernized may regain much of its character given the same treatment. Architectural detail (skirting boards, architraves and dadoes) and table tops make good subjects. Mantelpieces can also look stunning with a stone finish such as granite, but make sure the shape is appropriate – simple forms are best – or your illusion will not convince.

Contemporary designer interiors often include the more understated stone finishes, such as granite and sandstone, alongside wall finishes. This produces stunning results and is the ideal backdrop for many ethnic or craft-based *objets d'art*. Such professional looks are easy if you stick to the more straightforward techniques and classic looks. However, stone finishes can also be employed for much simpler ends. The rustic effect of the terracotta technique may be used in country interiors to evoke memories of Mediterranean interiors, even in the bleakest climate. It can be applied to all sorts of surfaces and will work especially

Left: A fireplace at Charleston Farm House, country home to some of London's Bloomsbury set. The granite effect, which is rougher than that of my recipe (see p. 152), may have been created with layers of daubed paint. It is a fine example of the Bloomsbury style.

Below: A fantasy stone effect very like the granite finish (see p. 152): this time for a wall beneath faux panelling. It works well in a period home, but also looks good in a more contemporary setting.

well on garden furniture and ornaments. Garden rooms and conservatories are also good projects for a restrained finish such as sandstone, which provides a lovely backdrop to foliage and flowers.

Professionals often apply stone effects to gessoed surfaces for an extra-flat finish, but this is not essential if the surface is sound and you prepare it well; and most of these recipes use water-based paints. That always increases the number of surfaces to which a technique can be applied, and their ease of application means a perfect surface is unnecessary.

Rich finishes, such as porphyry and lapis lazuli, are ultimate fantasy techniques and can be put to wild, wonderful uses. Their deep colours create a theatrical look best undertaken on the small scale and give found objects instant age and value. Indeed, many stone finishes are ideal for small items: apply them to lamp bases and candlesticks for grand, antique effects or mix them with ornamental techniques such as gilding (see p. 180). All of them can be applied to a variety of surfaces. Study the colour code at the head of each entry and check the key on page 41.

MARBLING

Marbling is perhaps the most well used of the stone finishes. It is possible, with careful study and practice, to reproduce accurate copies of any specific type, but in these recipes I show you how to create two *faux* or fantasy marbles. The method is less complicated and there is more room for artistic licence. However, even here a successful result depends on not overdoing the technique. And for 'authenticity' use picture references of real marble as a guide. Before you begin, decide on a basic pattern for the veining and other markings – it may be governed by the surface on which you are working – and keep the tones of your glazes close. Too much contrast makes for unconvincing results.

BASIC RECIPE – GREY FANTASY MARBLE

INGREDIENTS

Base coat ▶ 500ml white low-odour eggshell paint / 2tbsp neutral grey artists' oil colour

First glaze coat ▶ 375ml premixed, oil-based scumble glaze (transparent) / 3tbsp zinc white artists' oil colour / 200ml white spirit (approx.)

Second glaze coat ▶ 375ml premixed, oil-based scumble glaze / 2tbsp neutral grey artists' oil colour / 1tbsp zinc white artists' oil colour / 200ml white spirit (approx.)

First veining ▶ 1tbsp black artists' oil colour / $^{1}/_{2}$tbsp white spirit

Second veining ▶ 1tbsp yellow ochre artists' oil colour / $^{1}/_{2}$tbsp white spirit

Sealant ▶ 500ml clear satin polyurethane varnish / 50g (1$^{3}/_{4}$oz) french chalk

EQUIPMENT

3 large and 2 small containers for mixing paint and glaze / 2 x 50mm (2in) household brushes / 2 x 25mm (1in) household brushes / badger softener or lily-bristle brush / fitch / swordliner or fine artists' brush / cloth

INSTRUCTIONS

Base coat

ALWAYS WORK IN A WELL-VENTILATED AREA

1 Pour the eggshell paint into one of the large containers. Add the neutral grey and stir well.

2 Apply an even coat (see p. 34) to your prepared surface with one of the 50mm (2in) household brushes and allow to dry (24 hours).

First glaze coat

1 Pour the oil-based scumble into a second large container. Add the zinc white and 150ml white spirit (a little at a time), stirring well.

2 Apply to the base coat in diagonal, random strokes with one of the 25mm (1in) household brushes, allowing about a quarter of the base coat to show through.

3 Skim lightly over the glaze with the badger softener (or lily-bristle brush) to soften the brush strokes (see p. 34).

4 Using the fitch, flick some of the remaining white spirit onto the surface. Your aim is to disperse or spread the glaze a little, giving more depth to the effect.

Second glaze coat

1 Pour the oil-based scumble into a third large container. Add the neutral grey, zinc white, and 150ml white spirit (a little at a time), and stir well.

2 With the other 25mm (1in) household brush, apply the second glaze randomly to some of the areas not covered by the first glaze coat. When you have finished, you should still be able to see parts of the base coat.

3 Repeat the softening process and again flick some of the remaining white spirit onto the glaze.

First veining

1 Place the black oil colour in one of the small containers. Add the white spirit (a little at a time) and stir well.

2 Using the swordliner (or fine artists' brush) to apply the solution, make a series of small, twisting lines on the wet glaze. Work diagonally across the surface but try to vary the path of each vein. Make some of them travel vertically, add 'branches' here and there, and continue them from one side of the surface to the other. It is important to avoid too uniform an effect if you want to achieve an authentic look.

❶ GREY MARBLE
The final stage of the basic recipe is about to begin: the veining stages are complete and the effect has been softened with a lily-bristle brush.

Sample A shows the first glaze stage: white glaze has been applied to some areas but parts of the base coat still show through. The glaze has been softened and then dispersed.

Sample B shows the second, darker glaze and first veining. Now black and white blend to produce authentic two-tone veins.

A

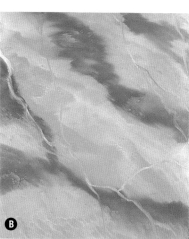

B

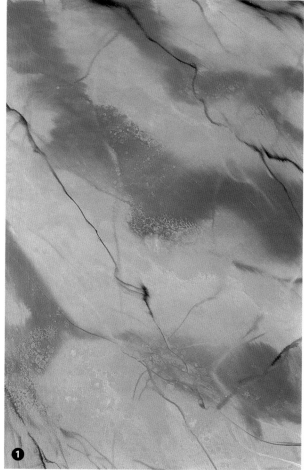

❶

The panelling in this room has been marbled using natural, sandy tones. It is complemented by the lovely candle sconce, antique paintings and overall period look. This is a handsome demonstration of how successful and authentic a marble finish can be.

Second veining

1 Place the yellow ochre in the other small container. Add the white spirit (a little at a time) and stir well.

2 Create more veins – these should be smaller and fewer than the black veins of the previous stage.

3 Skim lightly over the yellow ochre veins with the softener. Allow to dry (24 hours).

Sealant coat

1 Apply one coat of varnish with the other 50mm (2in) household brush and allow to dry for 12 hours.

2 Sprinkle the french chalk onto the partially dry surface and buff up with a cloth – this helps to give the 'cloudy' appearance typical of real marble.

VARIATION – BLACK AND GOLD FANTASY MARBLE

INGREDIENTS

Base coat ▶ 500ml black low-odour eggshell paint

First glaze coat ▶ 250ml premixed, oil-based scumble glaze (transparent) / 3tbsp zinc white artists' oil colour / 1tbsp oxide of chromium artists' oil colour / 200ml white spirit

Second glaze coat ▶ 250ml oil-based scumble glaze / 2tbsp zinc white artists' oil colour / 1tbsp yellow ochre artists' oil colour / 200ml white spirit

First veining ▶ 1tbsp premixed, oil-based scumble glaze / 1tbsp zinc white artists' oil colour / 1tbsp white spirit

Second veining ▶ 1tbsp oil-based scumble glaze / $^{1}/_{2}$tbsp zinc white artists' oil colour / $^{1}/_{2}$tbsp yellow ochre artists' oil colour / 1tbsp white spirit

Protective coat ▶ 500ml clear satin polyurethane or dead flat varnish

EQUIPMENT

2 x 50mm (2in) household brushes / 2 large and 2 small containers for mixing glaze / 2 x 25mm (1in) household brushes / badger softener or lily-bristle brush / fitch / swordliner or fine artists' brush / cloth

INSTRUCTIONS

Base coat

ALWAYS WORK IN A WELL-VENTILATED AREA

Stir the eggshell paint well and apply an even coat (see p. 34) to your prepared surface with one of the 50mm (2in) household brushes. Allow to dry (24 hours).

First and second glaze coats

Follow the method in Basic recipe, First and Second glaze coats, again adding only 150ml white spirit to the scumble and reserving the remaining 50ml to soften the glazes.

First and second veining

Follow the method in Basic recipe, First and Second veining, adding the oil colour and white spirit to the scumble.

Protective coat

Apply one coat of varnish with the other 50mm (2in) household brush and allow to dry (24 hours).

❷ BLACK AND GOLD MARBLE Bolder, more fantastic effects are a possibility with this type of finish, and the opportunity for experiment and colour variation is enormous. The glazes used here are thinner than those of the basic recipe and the result is a more translucent finish.

LAPIS LAZULI

It is easy to see why lapis lazuli, with its marvellous colouring sparkling with real gold, is known as the heaven stone. A rare, expensive mineral, it has been simulated for centuries. This finish looks good in traditional and contemporary interiors, but as spatter is a notoriously difficult technique to keep consistent it is best used over small areas. I use oil-based products because the glazes can be worked longer for softer effects. However, the best ultramarine oil colour is expensive – it uses lapis ground to pigment form. Cobalt blue is an adequate substitute.

BASIC RECIPE – LAPIS LAZULI

INGREDIENTS

Base coat ▶ 500ml white low-odour eggshell paint
First glaze coat ▶ 500ml premixed, oil-based scumble glaze (transparent) / 3 tbsp ultramarine blue artists' oil colour / 4tbsp white spirit
Second glaze coat ▶ 250ml premixed, oil-based scumble glaze / 2 tbsp black artists' oil colour / 2tbsp white spirit
First spatter coat ▶ 2tbsp premixed, oil-based scumble glaze / 1tbsp white artists' oil colour / 2tbsp white spirit
Second spatter coat ▶ 2tbsp premixed, oil-based scumble glaze / 1tbsp yellow ochre artists' oil colour / 2tbsp white spirit
Third spatter coat ▶ 2tbsp gold paint
Protective coat ▶ 500ml clear satin polyurethane varnish

EQUIPMENT

2 x 50mm (2in) household brushes / 2 large and 3 small containers for mixing glaze and for paint / 2 x 25mm (1in) household brushes / badger softener or lily-bristle brush / 3 fitches

INSTRUCTIONS

ALWAYS WORK IN A WELL-VENTILATED AREA

Base coat

Stir the eggshell paint well and apply an even coat (see p. 34) to the surface, using one of the 50mm (2in) household brushes. Allow to dry (24 hours).

First glaze coat

1 Pour the oil-based scumble into one of the large containers. Add the ultramarine blue and white spirit (a little at a time) and stir well.
2 Using one of the 25mm (1in) household brushes, apply to the surface with large, diagonal, brush strokes, allowing small areas of the base coat to show through. This ultramarine coat will remain the dominant colour.

Second glaze coat

1 Pour the oil-based scumble into the other large container. Add the black oil colour and white spirit (a little at a time) and stir well.
2 With the other 25mm (1in) household brush, apply glaze to the small areas of base coat still visible, again working diagonally across the surface.

1

① LAPIS LAZULI
This sample shows the finish created using the basic recipe. But note that the colouring of real lapis varies enormously and much paler or much redder stones are also found. Study the real thing (or picture references) before mixing your colour. Small boxes, candlesticks and lamp bases are all ideal subjects.

3 Soften both glazes by skimming the badger softener (or lily-bristle brush) lightly over the surface. Take care not to overdo it or you may begin to drag them.

First spatter coat

1 Pour the oil-based scumble into one of the small containers. Add the white oil colour and white spirit (a little at a time) and stir well.

2 Load one of the fitches with glaze. Holding a dry, clean fitch in one hand and the loaded brush in the other, tap the handle of the loaded brush against the handle of the other brush so that flecks of paint spatter the painted surface in a fine mist of dots (see p. 36). You are not aiming for an even coverage – spatter some areas more heavily than others. The less paint on the brush the finer the mist will be.

Second spatter coat

1 Pour the oil-based scumble into a second small container. Add the yellow ochre and white spirit (a little at a time) and stir well.

2 Load a second fitch with glaze and apply another fine mist of dots to the surface, using the same random technique as described above.

Third spatter coat

Pour the gold paint into a third small container – the little pots in which it is usually sold are hard to manage. Load a third fitch with paint and, again using the same technique, apply a very fine spatter coat to the surface. It is this coat that creates the 'fool's gold' effect typical of lapis lazuli – take care not to overdo it. Allow to dry (24 hours).

Protective coat

Apply one coat of varnish with the other 50mm (2in) household brush and allow to dry (24 hours).

SANDSTONE

This is a good place to start when first attempting stone finishes as the soft tones of sandstone are easy to simulate. The effect is subtle and you can apply it to a variety of surfaces. My recipe uses water-based paints, which make this a quick, easy technique that is both tough and resilient. A sandstone finish on walls is an excellent way to create an understated look that still brings atmosphere and character to a room, and it is often used as a basis for stone blocking (see p. 94). Bathrooms and hallways are ideal for the sandstone effect, and it is also an attractive finish for garden furniture and ornaments.

BASIC RECIPE – SANDSTONE

INGREDIENTS

Base coat ▶ 500ml white vinyl matt emulsion / 2tbsp raw sienna artists' acrylic colour

First glaze coat ▶ 500ml white vinyl matt emulsion / 2tbsp raw sienna acrylic artists' colour / 2tbsp water / methylated spirits (see instructions)

Second glaze coat ▶ 500ml white vinyl matt emulsion / $^{1}/_{2}$tbsp neutral grey artists' acrylic colour / 2tbsp water / methylated spirits

Third glaze coat ▶ 500ml white vinyl matt emulsion / 2tbsp water / methylated spirits

Protective coat ▶ 500ml clear satin acrylic varnish

EQUIPMENT

1 x 50mm (2in) emulsion brush / 4 containers for mixing paint and glaze / 4 sea sponges / water to dampen sponges / flower mister / 1 x 50mm (2in) varnish brush

INSTRUCTIONS
Base coat

1 Pour the emulsion into one of the containers. Add the raw sienna and stir well.
2 Brush an even coat (see p. 34) onto your prepared surface, using the emulsion brush, and allow to dry (2–3 hours).

First glaze coat

1 Pour the emulsion into a second container. Add the raw sienna and water (a little at a time) and stir well.

❶ SANDSTONE
The sample shows the effect on flat, wooden surfaces, but architectural features and plaster statues are also excellent subjects.

Here the sandstone finish is used on two surfaces for a little garden table. The top is MDF, and the pillar-style base is heavy-duty plastic. Both were well prepared (see pp. 43 and 47) before the finish was applied and are protected with two coats of satin polyurethane varnish.

2 Immerse one of the sponges in water and wring out. Apply the glaze to the base coat with the damp sponge in light, dabbing movements (see p. 35).

3 Half fill the flower mister with methylated spirits and spray the surface with a fine mist to disperse or spread the glaze slightly. This adds depth to the final effect.

4 Sponge the surface again, using a second damp sponge.

Second glaze coat

1 Pour the emulsion into a third container. Add the neutral grey and water (a little at a time) and stir well.

2 Using a third damp sponge, dab the glaze onto the still damp surface, carefully blending the two colours.

3 Spray another mist of methylated spirits onto the surface and allow to dry (2 hours).

Third glaze coat

1 Pour the emulsion into a fourth container. Add the water (a little at a time) and stir well.

2 Apply to the surface, using a fourth damp sponge in light, dabbing movements.

3 Spray with methylated spirits and allow to dry (2 hours).

Protective coat

Apply one coat of varnish, using the varnish brush, and allow to dry (2–3 hours).

Exterior use Substitute two coats of satin polyurethane varnish for protection, allowing 24 hours for each coat to dry.

PORPHYRY

Found all over the world, real porphyry is often used for pillars and architraves and sometimes fireplaces. English porphyry is a rich red, in France it may be green or pale purple, and in Denmark and Sweden it often contains pink and granite veining. Like other stone effects, the paint finish is built up with a series of spatter coats to create a granular effect, and it also gives the illusion of porphyry's varied colouring. The look brings grandeur to any interior. However, it can be oppressive and, as spatter is also difficult to control consistently, it is wisest to use this finish only on small areas. My recipe employs faster-drying water-based products, but traditionally, oil-based paints and glazes were used.

This plaster head was painted using the method described in the basic recipe. The rich, deep colour and intense tone suit the classical subject. Displayed outside, it would need heavier protection: substitute two coats of satin polyurethane varnish. You can try varying the colouring of the spatter coats for a different type of porphyry.

BASIC RECIPE – DEEP RED

INGREDIENTS

Base coats ▶ 1 litre premixed deep red emulsion paint
Glaze coat ▶ 250ml acrylic scumble glaze (transparent) / 3tbsp cadmium red artists' acrylic colour / 1tbsp raw umber artists' acrylic colour / 150ml water / methylated spirits (see instructions)
First spatter coat ▶ 1tbsp burnt umber artists' acrylic colour / 1tbsp water
Second spatter coat ▶ 1tbsp yellow ochre artists' acrylic colour / 1tbsp water
Third spatter coat ▶ 1tbsp zinc white artists' acrylic colour / 1tbsp water
Protective coat ▶ 500ml clear satin acrylic varnish

EQUIPMENT

2 x 50mm (2in) emulsion brushes / 1 large and 3 small containers for mixing paint and glaze / flower mister / 3 fitches / 1 x 50mm (2in) varnish brush

INSTRUCTIONS

Base coats

Stir the deep red emulsion paint well and apply two even coats (see p. 34) to your prepared surface with one of the emulsion brushes, allowing 2–3 hours for each coat to dry.

Glaze coat

1 Pour the acrylic scumble into the large container. Add the cadmium red, raw umber, and water (a little at a time) and stir well.

2 Using the other emulsion brush, apply with random strokes (see p. 34) to cover the base coat completely.

3 Half fill the flower mister with methylated spirits. Spray a fine mist over the surface to disperse or spread the glaze slightly – this will create more depth.

First spatter coat

1 Place the burnt umber in one of the small containers. Add the water (a little at a time), stirring well.

2 Load one of the fitches with glaze. Holding a dry fitch in one hand and the loaded fitch in the other, tap the handle of the loaded brush against the handle of the other brush – your aim is to spatter a fine spray of dots onto the still wet glaze (see p. 36).

Second spatter coat

1 Place the yellow ochre in a second small container. Add the water (a little at a time), stirring well.

2 Loading a second fitch, repeat the spatter process as described above.

Third spatter coat

1 Place the zinc white in a third small container. Add the water (a little at a time), stirring well.

2 Once more repeat the spatter process, loading a third fitch. Allow to dry (2 hours).

Protective coat

Apply one coat of varnish, using the varnish brush, and allow to dry (2–3 hours).

❶ DEEP RED
The rich tones of the basic recipe: a good example of how the finish appears on a flat, vertical surface. The different spatter colours – this is the easiest way to reproduce the granular quality of the stone – can be clearly seen.

GRANITE

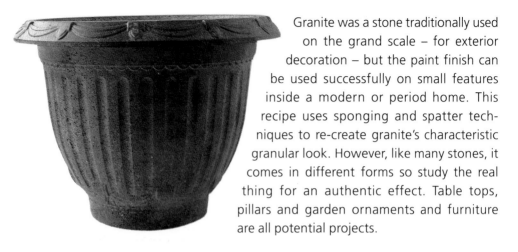

Granite was a stone traditionally used on the grand scale – for exterior decoration – but the paint finish can be used successfully on small features inside a modern or period home. This recipe uses sponging and spatter techniques to re-create granite's characteristic granular look. However, like many stones, it comes in different forms so study the real thing for an authentic effect. Table tops, pillars and garden ornaments and furniture are all potential projects.

BASIC RECIPE – GRANITE

INGREDIENTS

Base coat ▸ 500ml white vinyl matt emulsion / 2tbsp neutral grey artists' acrylic colour

First glaze coat ▸ 100ml white vinyl matt emulsion / 2tbsp neutral grey artists' acrylic colour / 1tbsp burnt umber artists' acrylic colour / 2tbsp water / methylated spirits (see instructions)

Second glaze coat ▸ 100ml white vinyl matt emulsion / 2tbsp water / methylated spirits

First spatter coat ▸ 1tbsp mars black artists' acrylic colour / 1tbsp water

Second spatter coat ▸ 1tbsp zinc white artists' acrylic colour / 1tbsp water / methylated spirits

Protective coat ▸ 500ml clear satin acrylic varnish

EQUIPMENT

3 large and 2 small containers for mixing paint and glaze / 1 x 50mm (2in) emulsion brush / 3 sea sponges / water to dampen sponges / flower mister / 2 fitches / 1 x 50mm (2in) varnish brush

INSTRUCTIONS

Base coat

1 Pour the emulsion into one of the large containers. Add the neutral grey and stir well.

2 Apply evenly (see p. 34) to your prepared surface, using the 50mm (2in) emulsion brush. Allow to dry (2–3 hours).

First glaze coat

1 Pour the emulsion into a second large container. Add the neutral grey, burnt umber, and water (a little at a time) and stir well.

2 Immerse one of the sponges in water and wring out. Using the damp sponge, apply glaze to the entire surface in light, dabbing movements (see p. 35).

3 Half fill the flower mister with methylated spirits and spray a fine mist over the surface. This causes the glaze to disperse or spread slightly, producing a more interesting texture. Allow to dry (2 hours).

Above left: This tub, made of heavy-duty plastic, was bought cheaply at a garden centre and painted as described in the recipe. Its basic shape recalls that of a traditional garden urn so it makes an ideal subject for a stone effect, and the finish disguises the fussy detail on the lip of the original (see p. 47).

Second glaze coat

1 Pour the emulsion into a third large container. Add the water (a little at a time), stirring well.

2 Apply to the entire surface with a second damp sponge in the same way.

3 Again using the flower mister, spray methylated spirits onto the glazed surface.

4 While the glaze is still wet, sponge again, using a third damp sponge, and carefully blend the two colours.

First spatter coat

1 Place the mars black in one of the small containers. Add the water (a little at a time) and stir well.

2 Load one of the fitches with glaze. Holding a clean fitch in one hand and the loaded fitch in the other, tap the handle of the loaded brush against the handle of the other so that flecks of paint spatter onto the surface (see p. 36). You are aiming for a fine haze of dots, applied more densely in some areas than in others.

Second spatter coat

1 Place the zinc white in the other small container. Add the water (a little at a time) and stir well.

2 Again spatter the surface with fine dots, using the second fitch and aiming for a random, uneven effect.

3 Using the flower mister, spray a fine mist of methylated spirits over the surface. Allow to dry (2 hours).

Protective coat

Apply one coat of varnish, using the varnish brush, and allow to dry (2–3 hours).

Exterior use Substitute two coats of satin polyurethane varnish for protection, allowing 24 hours for each coat to dry.

❶ GRANITE
The effect of the basic recipe on a flat surface: this finish would work well on panelling or on a table top. You could also try it on a plain, formal mantelpiece or fire surround.

TERRACOTTA

Terracotta's chalky look is popular and widely used for garden containers. However, some of the largest pots are expensive and, because they have a limited lifespan, the possibility of creating durable reproductions is attractive. Authenticity is achieved with simple dripping and sponging techniques: work the surface hard to enhance the effect. Objects with detail are especially successful because you can add extra ageing in the crevices. This finish is perfect for containers, but works well on surfaces and objects in kitchens or garden rooms too.

BASIC RECIPE – TERRACOTTA

INGREDIENTS

First base coat ▶ 500ml white vinyl matt emulsion / 2tbsp yellow ochre artists' acrylic colour / 1tbsp raw sienna artists' acrylic colour
Second base coat ▶ 500ml white vinyl matt emulsion / 2tbsp venetian red artists' acrylic colour / 2tbsp raw umber artists' acrylic colour / 1tbsp bronze ochre artists' acrylic colour
Glaze coat ▶ 100ml white vinyl matt emulsion / 150ml water

EQUIPMENT

3 containers for mixing paint and glaze / 2 x 50mm (2in) emulsion brushes / stippling or block brush / water to dampen brush and sponge / 1 x 25mm (1in) round fitch / sea sponge

INSTRUCTIONS
First base coat

1 Pour the emulsion into one of the containers. Add the yellow ochre and raw sienna and stir well.
2 Apply evenly (see p. 34) to your prepared surface with a 50mm (2in) emulsion brush. Leave to dry (2–3 hours).

Second base coat

1 Pour the emulsion into a second container. Add the venetian red, raw umber and bronze ochre and stir well.
2 Apply to the surface, using the other 50mm (2in) emulsion brush, with random strokes (see p. 34), allowing some of the base coat to show through. Leave to dry (2–3 hours).

❶ TERRACOTTA
Here the terracotta finish is applied to a flat surface and a three-dimensional detail (a plaster shape from a ceiling rose). Note how ageing on the irregular areas adds to the weathered effect. Plaster and plastic are ideal surfaces for the terracotta finish.

Three plastic pots were prepared and painted using the technique described in the basic terracotta recipe. They were finished with two coats of satin polyurethane varnish and sunk into the wet plaster of a roughly textured wall colourwashed (see p. 52) in a soft pink. Masonry nails driven through the back of the pots into the wall will give extra security.

Glaze coat

1 Pour the emulsion into a third container. Add the water (a little at a time), stirring well.

2 Dip the stippling (or block) brush in water and, with a light, tapping action, dampen the painted surface.

3 Hold or place the object in an upright position. Using the fitch, drip the glaze vertically down the surface – you are imitating the action of weathering. Repeat to cover the surface.

4 Immerse the sponge in water and wring out. Dab it lightly over the glaze to take up the excess water as the surface begins to dry to a chalky finish. Allow to dry (2 hours).

Exterior use Finish with two coats of satin polyurethane varnish, allowing 24 hours for each coat to dry.

METAL FINISHES

Left: These kitchen cupboards are either real metal finished with a dark rust technique (see p. 160) or an iron effect (see p. 166) given a later rust treatment. Either way, they demonstrate the versatility of metal finishes in a contemporary setting.

Metal is once more a fashionable element in interior design. From candlesticks to couches, expensive metal objects are much sought after so mastering these paint finishes can be an important part of your repertoire. Whether you want a contemporary look or one of aged beauty, the effect can be subtle or dramatic.

Salvage yards and junk shops are good sources for unusual and inexpensive objects to paint. Cheap metals can be transformed by using metal finishes to age them, and important but undistinguished fittings such as door handles and drawer pulls can easily be given more character. Larger items, such as chandeliers, lamps and lanterns, look amazing with a metal finish, making a room both impressive and individual. A hallway, for example, can look exceedingly grand hung with painted lamps and sconces. Old chairs and tables can be made to look as if they are metal, giving them real style and opulence. Verdigris is a lovely

Below: This interesting collection of shallow pots and vessels has been transformed with a lead-type finish (see p. 164). All suggest ideas for ways of using the lead technique on surfaces other than metal. Note how gilding (see p. 180) can complement the effect.

effect to use on a variety of surfaces: plain terracotta tubs and pots look quite wonderful treated with this finish – just as though they have been found on some archaeological site. Remember that with all these techniques the degree of ageing is up to you; reworking and repeating stages only adds to the effect.

With metal finishes you can adapt new items for a period home or, if you wish, create a fantasy period setting. If you want a medieval or Tudor look, go for the iron or lead finishes and, perhaps, try some of the much simpler and safer modern techniques for cold patination on new metal candlesticks or sconces. The rust effect is also good for either period and a natural for outside use. For a lighter, baroque style, try verdigris or softer cold-patination effects – verdigris on skirting boards and dado rails is an imaginative way to inject an aged effect.

Garden furniture and railings are good subjects for metal finishes. Gloss paint is the predictable choice for railings, but it can sometimes lack character; verdigris or rust are more atmospheric and appealing alternatives. Plastic and plaster garden tubs and troughs take metal finishes so well you may want to bring them indoors.

Metal finishes are mostly recommended for use on small areas, but it is possible to apply them to larger surfaces, such as panelling. This modern approach works well in contemporary interiors. A rust finish on kitchen units, for example, is an exciting option given a sophisticated, urban setting. Doors also make interesting projects and always add a highly individual look to a room.

My advice is: experiment. The more you do, the bolder you become. Remember that these finishes can be applied to various surfaces. Study the colour codes at the head of each entry and check the key on page 41.

Left: A splendid example of natural rusting on an old French clock: simulating such effects is not difficult using the rust recipe (see p. 160), but study natural ageing and weathering before you begin and remember that understatement works best.

Below: The lovely lines of this iron, period staircase could be darkened for greater emphasis. Apply a rust inhibitor (which also darkens the metal) and then rub in one coat of iron paste or black wax tinted with graphite powder.

PATINATION

When exposed to the elements metal fittings and architectural details tarnish and corrode over time. The results are often beautiful, evoking a wonderful sense of history, and craftsmen have now developed ways of reproducing patination on new metal. Some methods are complex and use dangerous chemicals, but cold-patination fluids (available for a variety of metals) are less dangerous, easier to use and create natural effects. Try experimenting with inexpensive candlesticks: the results can be effective. The key to success is timing – the process works very quickly – but it is a lot easier than waiting years for an object to age naturally or burying it in the garden. While these fluids are not as dangerous as most chemical methods, they are still toxic, so take care.

BASIC RECIPE – COLD PATINATION ON BRASS

INGREDIENTS

300ml methylated spirits / 200ml brown cold-patination fluid for brass, copper and bronze
Optional protective coat ▶ 200ml clear wax or oil fixative

EQUIPMENT

Cottonwool balls / water for rinsing / rubber gloves / protective mask / wirewool / rags (optional)

INSTRUCTIONS

WEAR GLOVES AND MASK WHEN USING COLD-PATINATION FLUIDS. FOLLOW MANUFACTURER'S INSTRUCTIONS AND WORK IN A WELL-VENTILATED AREA.

1 Clean the surface with cottonwool balls soaked in methylated spirits. Rinse in water and allow to dry (2 hours).

2 Put on the rubber gloves and protective mask. Rub clean cottonwool balls soaked in cold-patination fluid over the entire surface. It works very quickly – you will see the metal change colour as the fluid goes on. Rinse the surface in fresh water as soon as you have the colour you want. Leave it too long and it will be extremely dark. Never leave the fluid on for more than 2 minutes.

❸ ON COPPER
Another patination fluid gives an authentic verdigris effect in seconds. Again follow the basic recipe, applying the fluid with cottonwool or stippling it on with a soft brush. A second coat gives a more 'crusty' feel.

❶ ON BRASS
The basic method: only the middle of this sample is worked with wirewool, leaving the softer, aged effect at the edges.

❷ ON STEEL
This shows the use of the black cold-patination fluid for steel and iron. Simply follow the quantities and method given in the basic recipe.

3 As soon as you have rinsed the surface, rub it gently with the wirewool to remove the colour until you have the effect you want. Rinse in fresh water and allow to dry (1 hour).

Notes For a more hardwearing finish, rub wax (or oil fixative) over the entire surface with rags and allow to dry (1 hour).
Exterior use Apply one coat of oil fixative to the surface in the method described above.

Instant ageing and antiquing: these inexpensive candlesticks and holders have been patinated with the fluids used in the basic recipe and samples.

RUST

Probably the most extreme of the metal finishes, this look of age and corrosion is very popular. My recipe, which uses water-based materials, is fast, safe and simple, and you can, of course, vary the technique to enhance the impression of age. For example, you can simply apply both coats more heavily, remembering that for authenticity the effect must be uneven. Or give the rust more texture by adding about 70g (2¹/₂oz) fine sand to the base coat. It works well on metal, but can be applied to various surfaces.

BASIC RECIPE – RUST

INGREDIENTS

Base coat ▶ 500ml premixed black vinyl matt emulsion / 2tbsp titanium white artists' acrylic colour / 2tbsp ultramarine blue artists' acrylic colour
First rust coat ▶ 100ml raw sienna artists' acrylic colour / 3tbsp venetian red artists' acrylic colour / 1tbsp burnt umber artists' acrylic colour / 1tbsp red oxide artists' acrylic colour
Second rust coat ▶ 100ml yellow ochre artists' acrylic colour / 2tbsp yellow oxide artists' acrylic colour / 1tbsp raw sienna artists' acrylic colour

EQUIPMENT

3 containers for mixing paint / 1 x 50mm (2in) emulsion brush / 2 x 25mm (1in) round fitches

INSTRUCTIONS
Base coat

1 Pour the emulsion into one of the containers. Add the titanium white and ultramarine and stir well.
2 Apply an even coat (see p. 34) to your prepared surface with the emulsion brush and allow to dry (2–3 hours).

❶ RUST
This inexpensive metal table was an ideal subject. Detail (as in the coat-of-arms, above left) always lends itself to the technique. Ageing has been increased with two applications to the top and rim.

First rust coat

1 Place the raw sienna, venetian red, burnt umber and red oxide in a second container and stir well.
2 Using one of the fitches, stipple or lightly dab the rust mix onto the surface with a gentle, tapping action (see p. 35). Allow a little of the base-coat colour to show through. Leave to dry (1 hour).

Second rust coat

1 Put yellow ochre, yellow oxide and raw sienna in a third container and stir.
2 Using the other fitch, again stipple the mix onto the surface. Apply this coat more heavily, although parts of the other coats must remain visible. Build up the colour in some areas to avoid a uniform finish. Allow to dry (1 hour).

Exterior use Finish with two coats of matt polyurethane varnish, allowing 24 hours for each coat to dry.

❶

VERDIGRIS

Verdigris is perhaps the most stunning of the weathering effects to be seen on metal, occurring naturally on copper and bronze in the characteristic streaks of salty, acidic greens and whites. Simulating this effect originally involved the use of extremely toxic chemicals and intense heat (see also the less hazardous cold-patination technique for verdigris explained on p. 158). However, this recipe uses water-based products so it is much safer and easier. You can increase the aged effect by working the surface over and over again: it is fun to experiment.

The finish can be applied to many surfaces so hunt out all sorts of unusual objects to work on. Anything with lots of detail will pick up the look wonderfully well, although the method works on a flat surface just as successfully. Look at the real thing on statues and metalwork which have been exposed to the elements for years.

This decorative weather-vane is a good example of the verdigris effect. It has added to the character of the piece and, as the vane would once have been used outdoors, verdigris is an obvious and appropriate choice.

BASIC RECIPE – VERDIGRIS

INGREDIENTS
Base coat ▶ 500ml blackboard paint or premixed black vinyl matt emulsion
First verdigris coat ▶ 2tbsp titanium white artists' acrylic colour / 2tbsp viridian green artists' acrylic colour / 4tbsp water / methylated spirits (see instructions)
Second verdigris coat ▶ 2tbsp titanium white acrylic artists' colour / 1tbsp yellow ochre artists' acrylic colour / 100ml water / methylated spirits
Sealant / finishing coat ▶ 500ml clear matt acrylic varnish / 25g ($^9/_{10}$oz) whiting or chalk powder

EQUIPMENT
1 x 50mm (2in) emulsion brush / 2 containers for mixing paint / 3 x 25mm (1in) round fitches / flower mister / 1 x 50mm (2in) varnish brush / rags

VERDIGRIS

INSTRUCTIONS
Base coat

Stir the blackboard or emulsion paint well and apply an even coat (see p. 34) to the entire surface, using the emulsion brush. Allow to dry (2–3 hours).

First verdigris coat

1 Place the titanium white and viridian green in one of the containers. Add the water (a little at a time) and stir well.
2 Load one of the fitches with the solution and, holding or positioning the object vertically, dribble the liquid onto the surface so it drips downwards. Repeat to cover the surface.
3 Half fill the flower mister with methylated spirits and spray a fine mist onto the surface to disperse the paint slightly.

Second verdigris coat

1 Place the titanium white and yellow ochre in the other container. Add 50ml water (a little at a time) and stir well.
2 Using a second fitch, dribble the solution in the same way.
3 Spray a fine mist of methylated spirits, as described above.
4 Dribble the remaining water onto the vertical surface as before, using a third fitch, until you have the effect you want. Allow to dry (2 hours).

Sealant / finishing coat

1 Brush one coat of varnish onto the entire surface, using the 50mm (2in) varnish brush, and leave to become tacky (approx. 20 minutes).
2 Rub in some whiting (or chalk powder), paying particular attention to any detail. This helps to give an authentic 'chalky' finish. Wipe off any loose, excess whiting with rags and allow to dry (2–3 hours).

Exterior use Add two coats of satin polyurethane varnish, allowing 24 hours for each coat to dry.

Opposite: This impressive lion-head fountain is, in fact, made of plastic, transformed by the use of the verdigris effect. It was prepared and primed with two coats of blackboard paint. To protect a surface from regular exposure to water, add two or three coats of yacht varnish after the sealant/ finishing coat, allowing 4–6 hours for each coat to dry.

❶ VERDIGRIS
The basic recipe applied to a flat surface and three-dimensional detail: you can, if you prefer, substitute 500ml premixed rust emulsion for blackboard paint in the base coat. The effect is similar.

LEAD

Aged, weathered lead has a grey-blue, salty or chalky appearance, the result of chemical changes in the metal. It is a look that is easily created with water-based products – simply by dripping coloured glazes onto a vertical surface and then ageing with whiting. Plastic flower pots and troughs are ideal subjects, but plain, cheap metal items are equally effective and will look wonderfully expensive. As with most of the metal effects, you choose how much to age the finish: I really enjoy working into the glazes to create an antique look.

BASIC RECIPE – LEAD

INGREDIENTS

Sealant coat ▶ 500ml PVA adhesive or white glue / 500ml water

Base coat ▶ 500ml white vinyl matt emulsion / 1tbsp burnt umber artists' acrylic colour / 1tbsp premixed black vinyl matt emulsion

First glaze ▶ 4tbsp premixed black vinyl matt emulsion / 2tbsp titanium white artists' acrylic colour / 1/2tbsp burnt umber artists' acrylic colour / 150ml water

Second glaze coat ▶ 5tbsp titanium white artists' acrylic colour / 2tbsp burnt umber artists' acrylic colour / 1tbsp ultramarine blue artists' acrylic colour / 150ml water

Sealant / finishing coat ▶ 500ml PVA adhesive or white glue / 500ml water / 50g (1³/₄oz) whiting or chalk powder

EQUIPMENT

5 containers for mixing paint and glaze / 2 x 25mm (1in) emulsion brushes / 3 x 50mm (2in) emulsion brushes / 1 x 25mm (1in) round fitch / rags

INSTRUCTIONS
Sealant coat

1 Pour the PVA adhesive (or white glue) into one of the containers. Add the water (a little at a time) and stir well.

2 Brush the solution onto your prepared surface, using one of the 25mm (1in) emulsion brushes. Allow to dry (1 hour).

Base coat

1 Pour the white emulsion into a second container. Add the burnt umber and black emulsion and stir well.

2 Apply evenly (see p. 34) to the surface with one of the 50mm (2in) emulsion brushes and allow to dry (2–3 hours).

❶ LEAD
The classic effect: highly successful on flat surfaces and relief detailing so you can, for example, convert cheap plastic into something a great deal more splendid. Success depends partly on finding an appropriate design.

PAINT RECIPES

The inexpensive metal sconce on the left of the picture has been changed beyond recognition by the application of the lead effect described in the basic recipe.

First glaze coat

1 Pour the emulsion into a third container. Add the white, burnt umber, and 100ml water (a little at a time). Stir well.
2 Apply the glaze to the entire surface with random strokes (see p. 34), using a second 50mm (2in) emulsion brush.
3 Load the fitch with water and, holding the object vertically, drip the liquid onto the surface so it runs from top to bottom. This helps to disperse the glaze, allowing some of the base to show through. Repeat to cover. Allow to dry (1 hour).

Second glaze coat

1 Put the titanium white, burnt umber and ultramarine in a fourth container. Add 100ml water (a little at a time) and stir.
2 Using a third 50mm (2in) brush, apply with random cross-hatched strokes. Parts of the other coats must remain visible.
3 Drip water onto the surface again. Allow to dry (2 hours).

Sealant / finishing coat

1 Put the PVA adhesive (or white glue) in a fifth container. Add the water (a little at a time) and stir well.
2 Apply to the entire surface with the other 25mm (1in) emulsion brush and leave until it is tacky (5–7 minutes).
3 Rub the whiting (or chalk powder) into the surface, using rags. Pay special attention to any detail. Remove excess whiting with clean rags. Allow to dry (2–3 hours).

Exterior use Add two coats of matt polyurethane varnish, allowing 24 hours for each coat to dry.

IRON

Iron was once associated mostly with outdoor objects, but its use in interiors is increasing and it can be stunning in both traditional and contemporary rooms. I have given you two ways of creating this effect. The addition of a 'rust' glaze in the basic recipe (see Second glaze coat) gives a look of natural patination, providing a greater feel of antiquity, but the variation has perhaps a subtler, less shiny appearance. These finishes need not be confined to metal objects: doors, skirtings and some architectural detailing are all good subjects. So are garden furniture and ornaments. Look in salvage yards and junk shops – some of my best, certainly most satisfying, finds have been in such places.

BASIC RECIPE – USING SILVER PAINT

INGREDIENTS
Base coat ▶ 500ml silver paint
First glaze coat ▶ 4tbsp premixed black vinyl matt emulsion / 2tbsp water
Second glaze coat ▶ 4tbsp titanium white artists' acrylic colour / 2tbsp venetian red artists' acrylic colour / 1tbsp burnt sienna artists' acrylic colour / 100ml water

EQUIPMENT
1 x 50mm (2in) emulsion brush / 2 containers for mixing glaze / sea sponge / water for sponge / 1 x 100mm (4in) flat brush / 1 x 25mm (1in) fitch

1 SILVER PAINT
The basic recipe on flat and detailed surfaces.

2 WAX AND POWDER
The variation has a darker, moodier effect. More easily controlled than the basic recipe, it is a good choice for any complex or large-scale project.

INSTRUCTIONS
Base coat

Stir the silver paint well and apply an even coat (see p. 34) to your prepared surface, using the emulsion brush. Allow to dry (2–3 hours).

First glaze coat

1 Pour the black emulsion into one of the containers. Add the water (a little at a time) and stir well.
2 Immerse the sponge in water and wring out. Apply the glaze to the entire surface with the damp sponge, using small, dabbing movements (see p. 35).
3 Soften the sponging by skimming the surface of the glaze with the flat brush. Allow to dry (2 hours).

PAINT RECIPES

Second glaze coat

1 Place the white, venetian red and burnt sienna in the other container. Add the water (a little at a time) and stir well.

2 Load the fitch with glaze and dribble it onto the surface, while holding or positioning the object so that the liquid drips downwards. Repeat until the entire surface has been treated. Allow to dry (2 hours).

This curious architectural detail, probably designed to crown the crest of a roof, is made of plaster. Found in a salvage yard, it seemed the perfect subject for the iron effect of the basic recipe. The natural patination of the old chain in the foreground demonstrates how convincing the finish is.

VARIATION – USING WAX AND POWDER

INGREDIENTS
Base coat ▶ 500ml blackboard paint
Wax coat ▶ 275ml black polish / 50g (1³/₄oz) silver metallic powder

EQUIPMENT
1 x 50mm (2in) emulsion brush / protective mask / container for mixing wax / rags / clean shoe brush

INSTRUCTIONS
Base coat
ALWAYS WEAR A MASK WHEN USING METALLIC POWDERS
Stir the blackboard paint well and brush an even coat (see p. 34) onto your prepared surface. Allow to dry (2 hours).

Wax coat
1 Put on the protective mask. Place 250ml polish and metallic powder in the container and mix well. If you want a darker tone, add more powder. Take care not to add too much or your polish will become crumbly and unmanageable.

2 Rub the wax into the entire surface, using rag in a downward action. Allow to dry (2 hours). Rub a little black polish into any over-silvery areas. Then buff up with the shoe brush.

Exterior use (both recipes) Finish with two coats of satin polyurethane varnish, allowing 24 hours for each coat to dry.

ORNAMENTAL FINISHES

Like all the stone finishes, most of these decorative effects are bravura or illusionary finishes; all of them are even more fanciful. Once dismissed as too time consuming or expensive to reproduce, modern paint technology has caused many of them to lose their mystique and become accessible to anyone prepared to experiment a little. Traditional oil- and water-gilding, for example, are complex techniques, but water-based sizes and the more robust Dutch metal leaf now widely available make the art of gilding attainable for all. Metallic powders, available in many colours, are also good for embellishing many surfaces. And the modern substitute for genuine lacquer, marketed as lacquer paint, gives an authentic look. Building up the finish still takes time and the paint, which has a high gloss content, dries slowly, but it is worth it to obtain the classic look.

These finishes are ideal for small items and areas of detail because, as with many bravura finishes, it is not easy to maintain consistency over a large area. Experimenting with colour and texture is important, because slight changes in tone and surface finish may make a lot of difference to the final effect. Unless your aim is total fantasy, try not to overdo these techniques – in scale or execution.

Stencilling is the exception here: it is not, of course, a fantasy finish and you can stencil entire walls to great effect. But no ornamental section would have seemed complete without it, and you can, if you wish, make fantastical bowers of bliss with vines or floral swags in a stencilled bedroom.

Great houses and stately homes are valuable sources of information for ornamental finishes. Look closely at some of the most decorated surfaces and you will find

Left: This delicate plaster shelf-sconce is a great subject for gilding (see p. 180). It was distressed by rubbing the finish down with wire-wool and methylated spirits to reveal the base material. The wall has been gessoed and aged with broken-colour techniques.

Below: A bathroom cupboard painted a contemporary shade of blue and enlivened with the imaginative use of gilding: the brightness of the gold has again been softened by ageing and distressing (see above).

that many of them are achieved with paint effects. It is not difficult to attain similar results in your own home using the recipes given in this section.

From the ancient art of Chinese lacquer to the wonderful richness of gilding and tortoiseshell, these finishes can be used to transform something plain into something of great beauty, and they can also add the final touch to any interior. Always watch out for the unusual shape or design that will take on a very different look once it has been painted. But beware: though some of these finishes could be used to restore or repair old objects, you must be sure that the piece will not suffer, rather than benefit, from your attention. Add, for example, a modern lacquer

finish to an antique oriental piece and you will seriously reduce its value.

Remember these finishes can be applied to various surfaces. Study the colour codes at the head of each entry and the key on page 41.

Above: A charming example of stencilling (see p. 184) shows how well the technique works as an alternative to wallpaper. The brown on stone combination, charged with hints of red, is ideal for a rustic kitchen.

Left: Stencilling again – this time within formal panels. The style and colouring are very reminiscent of Scandinavian interiors (see p. 131). The look has been given more authenticity by rubbing down the surface. Decorated and aged furniture (see p. 128) complete the effect.

LACQUER

Lacquering is over a thousand years old and originated in China, the only place where the tree *Rhus verniciflua* grew – its resin was the initial source of lacquer. This rich effect is traditionally achieved by applying layers of lacquer or high-gloss paint to build up a deep sheen: each coat is sanded and up to a hundred are applied. My recipe emulates (but abbreviates!) the finish, using oil-based paints. You can gild and paint the end product or apply bronze or gold powders to the wet coats for more lustre (see p. 27). Trays offer excellent scope for decoration.

BASIC RECIPE – DEEP RED

INGREDIENTS

Base coats ▶ 2¹/₂ litres synthetic gesso / 1¹/₄ litre water / 500ml amber shellac / 100ml methylated spirits

Lacquer ▶ 1¹/₂ litres flat red gloss paint / 4tbsp burnt umber artists' oil colour / 500ml clear gloss polyurethane varnish (one coat)

Decoration (optional) ▶ 150ml flat yellow gloss paint / 150ml flat black gloss paint

EQUIPMENT

3 containers for mixing gesso and paint / 4 x 25mm (1in) household brushes / fine wirewool / wet and dry paper / soapy water / rags

Decoration (optional) ▶ pencil / tracing paper / Chinagraph pencil / 2 x 25mm (1in) flat artists' brushes

INSTRUCTIONS

ALWAYS WORK IN A WELL-VENTILATED AREA

Base coats

1 Pour the synthetic gesso into one of the containers. Add the water (a little at a time) and stir well.

This chest may have been made in Northampton, Massachusetts in about 1724. Most colonial pieces were painted with solid colours; black and red were common. Designs in other colours were added for those who had more to spend. Signs of ageing can be seen all over the surface of this chest.

❶ DEEP RED
The basic recipe: the design on this sample is similar to that on the chest opposite. The pattern was drawn onto tracing paper, transferred to the surface with a Chinagraph pencil and then painted, using the artists' brushes. Two coats of each colour were applied, allowing 24 hours for each coat to dry.

❷ BLACK
Flat black gloss is used for the lacquer coats instead of red. The design was added as above, but 150ml flat red gloss paint was substituted for the black.

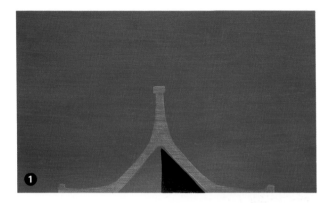

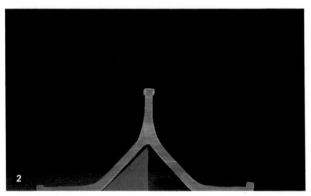

2 Apply an even coat to your prepared surface with one of the household brushes, using approx. 500ml of the solution. Allow to dry (2–3 hours).
3 Rub with wirewool and apply four more coats in the same way, rubbing down with wirewool after each one.
4 Place the shellac in a second container. Add the methylated spirits (a little at a time) and stir well.
5 Apply an even coat to the gesso, using a second household brush. Allow to dry (2 hours).

Lacquer coats

1 Stir the red gloss well and apply an even coat to the entire surface (see p. 34) with a third household brush, using just under 500ml of paint. Allow to dry (24 hours).
2 Rub down gently with the wet and dry paper.
3 Wipe the surface clear of dust, using the soapy water and clean rags, and leave to dry (1 hour).
4 Using the same brush, apply two more coats of red gloss, repeating the sanding and cleaning steps after each one.
5 Pour the remaining gloss paint into a third container. Add the burnt umber and varnish (a little at a time) and stir well. Apply evenly with a fourth household brush and allow to dry (24 hours). Apply a second coat if required.

Notes To decorate see sample 1; apply before Lacquer, step 5.

TORTOISESHELL

This effect simulates the appearance of the shell of the sea turtle, which was first used as a decorative veneer in the East. Imitated by craftsmen for centuries, the pattern is created with a series of diagonal strokes on different background colours, such as white, cinnamon and gold. The latter was once real gold leaf but Dutch metal leaf or gold sprays are just as successful. This recipe reproduces the classic colours using water-based paints. It works well on small objects – flat surfaces are best as the shell cannot be carved – but it is striking on screens and table tops.

BASIC RECIPE – UMBER AND OCHRE

INGREDIENTS

Base coat ▶ 500ml white vinyl matt emulsion / 3tbsp raw sienna artists' acrylic colour

Glaze coats ▶ 3tbsp yellow ochre artists' acrylic colour / 3tbsp raw sienna artists' acrylic colour / 3tbsp burnt umber artists' acrylic colour / 500ml acrylic scumble glaze (transparent) / 150ml water

Spatter coat ▶ 1tbsp burnt umber artists' acrylic colour / 3¹/₃tbsp water

Protective coat ▶ 500ml clear satin acrylic varnish

EQUIPMENT

Container for mixing paint / 1 x 50mm (2in) emulsion brush / 4 saucers for mixing glaze / 1 x 50mm (2in) household brush / 3 x 25mm (1in) flat artists' brushes / badger softener or lily-bristle brush / toothbrush / disposable gloves / 1 x 50mm (2in) varnish brush

INSTRUCTIONS

Base coat

1 Pour the emulsion into the container. Add the raw sienna and stir well.

2 Apply an even coat (see p. 34) to your prepared surface with the emulsion brush and allow to dry (2–3 hours).

An interesting example of the use of the tortoiseshell finish, the little lampshade blends delightfully with the surrounding objets d'art and antiques. The effect could easily be reproduced on a simple metal shade.

① UMBER AND OCHRE
The basic-recipe colourway: the sample is painted on an area larger than is normally undertaken, but it illustrates well the potential use of tortoiseshell on flat surfaces, such as small decorative panels or trays.

Glaze coats

1 Place each of the three colours on a separate saucer. Add 50ml acrylic scumble and 50ml water (a little at a time) to each colour and stir well. Set aside.

2 Apply the remaining 350ml acrylic scumble in a thin, even coat to the base coat, using the household brush.

3 Using one of the artists' brushes, apply the yellow ochre glaze to the surface in random, diagonal strokes. You are aiming for a rough, 'daubed' effect with much of the base coat still showing through.

4 Repeat the process, using a different brush for each of the remaining, darker colours. Brush glaze onto other random areas until the base coat is completely covered.

5 Skim lightly over the surface with the badger softener (or lily-bristle brush), allowing the hairs of the brush to touch the glaze (see p. 34). Your aim is to remove the brush strokes and to merge the colours into each other to create the tortoiseshell effect. Allow to dry (24 hours).

These simple boxes illustrate a variation of the basic recipe in colours often found in tortoiseshell. The base coat was a premixed deep red emulsion; in the glaze coats 3tbsp cadmium red replaced the yellow ochre; the spatter and protective coats were unchanged.

Spatter coat

1 Place the burnt umber on the fourth saucer. Add the water (a little at a time) and stir well.

2 Put on the disposable gloves. Load the toothbrush with paint. Holding it about 20cm (8in) from the surface, flick back the bristles with the fingers of your other hand to produce a fine mist of paint dots (see p. 36). You are aiming for little patches of dots rather than the even coverage typical of spattering. Allow to dry (4–5 hours).

Protective coat

Using the varnish brush, apply one coat of varnish and allow to dry completely (2–3 hours).

SHAGREEN

The name shagreen is of Turkish origin and the material has always had an exotic allure. It was primarily made from untanned sharkskin, and its characteristic small, granular pitting was created by trampling seeds into its surface when it was still moist and shaking them out when dry. The leather was then stained in a variety of different colours (including pink, grey and blue), although pale moss green has always been the most popular. Much loved in the Art Deco period, in these more ecologically sensitive times real shagreen is seen only on small luxury items, such as boxes, cigarette cases and lighters. My recipe simulates the material using oil-based paints and a simple water-on-oil technique that authentically reproduces its granular indentations.

BASIC RECIPE – PALE GREEN

INGREDIENTS	**Base coat ▶ 500ml white low-odour eggshell paint** **Glaze coat ▶ 250ml premixed oil-based scumble glaze (transparent) /** **2tbsp sap green artists' oil colour / 1tbsp zinc white artists' oil colour /** **150ml white spirit / 500ml water** **Protective coat ▶ 500ml clear satin polyurethane varnish**
EQUIPMENT	**1 x 25mm (1in) household brush / container for mixing glaze / 1 x 50mm** **(2in) household brush / stippling or block brush / flower mister / 1 x 25mm** **(1in) varnish brush**
INSTRUCTIONS	ALWAYS WORK IN A WELL-VENTILATED AREA
Base coat	Stir the eggshell paint well and apply an even coat (see p. 34) to your prepared surface with the 25mm (1in) household brush. Allow to dry (24 hours).
Glaze coat	**1** Pour the oil-based scumble into the container. Add the sap green and zinc white oil colours, and white spirit (a little at a time) and stir well. **2** Apply to the entire surface, in random strokes (see p. 34), using the 50mm (2in) household brush.

❶ PALE GREEN
This sample illustrates the basic recipe: the classic colour of shagreen.

❷ COBALT BLUE
A variation on the basic recipe: here the glaze coat is tinted with 2tbsp cobalt blue and 1tbsp zinc white.

❶

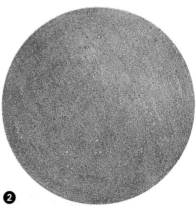

❷

The top of this small flower stand has been painted with a shagreen finish. It is an ideal subject and the finish works well with the dainty, gilded base, which has been treated with an ageing glaze of a similar tone (see p. 180).

3 Tap the surface of the glaze lightly with the stippling or block brush to eradicate the brush strokes (see p. 35).

4 Fill the flower mister with water and lightly spray a fine mist over the entire surface. Allow to dry (24 hours) – as the beads of water on the oily surface evaporate, they disperse or spread the paint slightly, making the small rings which create the shagreen effect.

Protective coat   Apply one coat of varnish to the surface, using the varnish brush, and allow to dry (6–8 hours).

LEATHER

Using leather stretched over a flat surface has been popular for many centuries. As a very hardwearing material, it covered chairs, screens, chests and table tops, and it was frequently stained with coloured dyes and embossed with decorative patterns. This recipe re-creates the sumptuous look of old leather and can also be used to decorate panels and frames. It is an easy technique, but it is important to establish a good textured base coat with a heavy and random application of emulsion paint. The rich colours are created by rubbing stained waxes into the rough surface, and again you must spread the wax evenly to achieve the characteristic look of real leather. This is a bold effect and, therefore, in the darkest colours may not be suitable for large areas, although in a library or living room full of antiques and *objets d'art* it would work superbly on great wall panels. On a smaller scale and in an alternative colourway, it looks good in modern interiors. Experiment with colour. Wherever this finish is used, the result is likely to be theatrical and a little grand.

BASIC RECIPE – BROWN

INGREDIENTS

Base coat ▶ 500ml white vinyl matt emulsion / 4tbsp raw sienna artists' acrylic colour
Wax coat ▶ 250ml clear wax / 2tbsp burnt umber artists' oil colour

EQUIPMENT

2 containers for mixing paint and wax / 1 x 75mm (3in) household brush / 1 x 25mm (1in) flat artists' brush / disposable gloves / soft lint-free cloths / fine sandpaper

INSTRUCTIONS
Base coat

1 Pour the emulsion into one of the containers. Add the raw sienna and stir well.
2 Load the household brush heavily with paint and apply to your prepared surface, using rough, random, circular strokes to build up a textured effect. Allow to dry (6 hours).

Wax coat

1 Place the wax in the other container. Add the burnt umber and stir well.
2 Apply an even coat to the entire surface, using the flat artists' brush.
3 Put on the disposable gloves. Using soft cloth, rub the wax into the surface with a circular action. Change the cloth frequently as it will quickly become clogged with wax. Allow to dry completely (24 hours).

Ageing

Rub lightly over the surface with the sandpaper for a more worn effect.

Above left: Gilt studs add a gothic touch to the leather finish on a picture frame. A variation on the basic recipe, the base coat was tinted with 2tbsp cobalt blue; 1¹/2tbsp ultramarine blue coloured the wax.

❶ BROWN
The classic colour: the basic colour-way is effective on tables and screens.

❷ DEEP RED
This colourway is very rich and would add grandeur to any room when used on a chest or screen. The base coat is tinted with 4tbsp cadmium red, and the wax with 2$\frac{1}{2}$tbsp cadmium red and $\frac{1}{2}$tbsp raw umber.

❸ DARK GREEN
The base coat is tinted with 3tbsp sap green; 3tbsp oxide of chromium green colour the wax coat.

❹ BLACK
Here the base-coat colour is created with 3tbsp neutral grey; then 2tbsp mars black tint the wax coat.

BRONZING

Bronzing is an ancient technique used as an alternative or supplementary method to gilding (see p. 180). An object or area is sized and a fine metallic powder, originally real gold, is brushed or blown onto it to produce a subtly bronzed, antique look. The powders are very fine and toxic so always wear a mask and take care. Try not to use too much at a time to avoid waste and mess. Many colours and tones are available: most tones of gold, bronze and copper are easily found and other colours, such as purple, green and red, can be bought in specialist shops.

Bronzing can be used on a variety of surfaces and many objects. The technique produces an opulent look that is great for transforming old or second-hand objects. Metal chairs and other garden ornaments are ideal. So, too, are plaster architectural mouldings and statues. It is also an excellent way of applying subtle decoration to lacquer (see p. 170) and other painted items. Just mask the areas you want to protect and follow the recipe, applying size as required. The powders tend to spread so do not use them on newly painted or varnished areas.

BASIC RECIPE – DEEP GOLD

INGREDIENTS

Base coat ▶ 250ml red oxide primer
Bronzing ▶ 250ml water-based size / 75g (2²/₃oz) deep gold bronze powder
Protective coat ▶ 250ml amber french enamel varnish

EQUIPMENT

2 x 25mm (1in) household brushes / protective mask / 1 x 25mm (1in) flat artists' brush / small, soft-bristled brush / soft cloths / 1 x 25mm (1in) varnish brush

❶ DEEP GOLD
The basic recipe: a rich, yet subtle effect.

❷ COPPER
This variation follows the basic recipe, simply sub-stituting copper bronze powder at the bronzing stage and red french enamel varnish for the protective coat.

❶   ❷

INSTRUCTIONS

ALWAYS WEAR A MASK AND WORK IN A WELL-VENTILATED AREA

Base coat

Stir the red oxide primer well and apply an even coat (see p. 34) to your prepared surface, using one of the household brushes. Allow to dry (24 hours).

Bronzing

1 Shake or stir the size according to the manufacturer's instructions. Apply a thin, even coat to the base coat, using

Bronzing a metal chair, following a variation of the basic recipe.

A rust inhibitor and metal primer were applied first (see p. 45), and then came two coats of premixed black oil-based primer (250ml each). Light gold bronze powder was stirred into the size at the bronzing stage, and the protective coat was a neutral french enamel varnish.

A final coat of satin polyurethane varnish was added for extra protection as the chair was to be used outside. It was allowed to dry for 24 hours.

the other household brush. Allow to become tacky and transparent (approx. 20–30 minutes).

2 Put on the protective mask. Using the artists' brush, take up a little of the bronze powder at a time and brush it carefully onto the surface until most of the base coat is covered.

3 Gently remove some of the excess powder with the soft-bristled brush.

4 Rub carefully with soft cloths to burnish.

Protective coat   Apply one coat of varnish to the surface, using the varnish brush, and allow to dry (1 hour).

GILDING

Real gold leaf is both costly and time consuming to use, and today there are a variety of alternatives (see p. 26). Dutch metal leaf is the most convincing, being also cheaper and simpler to apply, and the modern gold sizes – Italian (water-based) and Japan (oil-based) – are effective and faster drying than the traditional substances. To give a smooth surface for gilding, a gesso is traditionally applied, tinted red to give a good base colour to the leaf – gesso can be bought ready mixed or made from whiting mixed with PVA adhesive. But it is simpler and equally effective to substitute, as this recipe does, a coat of red oxide primer or deep red emulsion. Gilding is ideal for plaster mouldings, picture and mirror frames, candlesticks and a variety of other ornaments.

❶ CLASSIC AGEING
This plaster leaf is gilded using the Dutch metal leaf method described in the basic recipe. Here the ageing glaze is grey.

❷ OLD GOLD
The ageing glaze for this leaf is coloured with 2tbsp yellow ochre mixed with 1tbsp acra gold. This tone brings out the richness of the metal leaf and is reminiscent of the Italian gold used on many religious paintings.

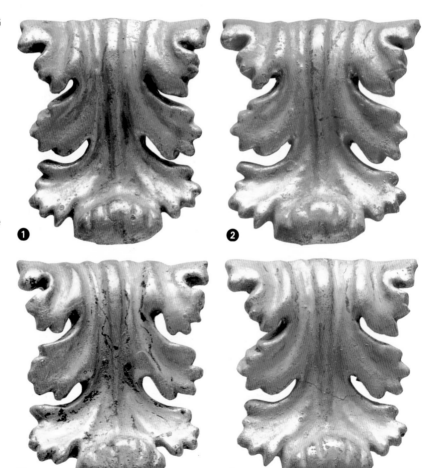

❸ PALE GOLD
The base coat is pre-mixed dark green vinyl matt emulsion. The ageing glaze is tinted with 1tbsp coeruleum blue and 1¹/2tbsp titanium white. The green base gives the gold a thinner tone.

❹ MODERN GOLD
This ageing glaze is simply coloured with 2tbsp dioxazine purple and is a more contemporary way of treating a gilded object.

BASIC RECIPE – GOLD DUTCH METAL WITH CLASSIC AGEING

INGREDIENTS

Base coat ▶ 250ml red oxide primer or deep red vinyl matt emulsion
Sizing coat ▶ 250ml Italian water-based or quick-drying Japan gold size
Gilding ▶ 12 gold Dutch metal leaves
Optional additional ageing ▶ 2tbsp methylated spirit
Sealant coat ▶ 250ml amber shellac
Ageing glaze ▶ 2tbsp white vinyl silk emulsion / $1/2$tbsp neutral grey artists' acrylic colour / $1/2$tbsp yellow ochre artists' acrylic colour / 2tbsp water

EQUIPMENT

3 x 25mm (1in) emulsion brushes / box or large bowl / disposable gloves / 1 x 25mm (1in) round, very soft-bristled brush / 2 soft polishing cloths / wirewool (optional) / 1 x 25mm (1in) varnish brush / container for mixing glaze / rags

INSTRUCTIONS
Base coat

Stir the primer (or emulsion) well and, using one of the emulsion brushes, apply an even coat (see p. 34) to your prepared surface. Allow to dry (2–3 hours).

Sizing coat

Shake or stir the size, following the manufacturer's instructions. Using a second emulsion brush, apply a thin but even coat of size to the entire surface. Never overload the brush because it is important to leave as few bubbles on the surface as possible. Allow the size to dry a little (20–30 minutes) until it becomes transparent and tacky.

Gilding

1 Place the box (or bowl) on your work surface with the metal leaves close at hand.
2 Put on the gloves and hold the object over the box to catch any broken leaf. Lift up each leaf and lay it carefully on the surface. Cover the object completely, or, for an aged effect, allow some of the primer to show through.
3 Use the soft-bristled brush to dust the object lightly, brushing the excess leaf into the box. You can use small pieces to cover gaps and keep larger ones for another project.
4 Rub the surface gently with one of the polishing cloths until it is smooth and shiny. Take care not to rub too hard or too much or the leaf will lift off.

Sealant coat

Using the varnish brush, apply a thin but even coat of shellac to the surface to deepen the colour. This is important as Dutch metal can look tinny. Leave to dry (45 minutes).

Ageing glaze

1 Pour the emulsion into the container and add the neutral grey and yellow ochre. Stir thoroughly and then add the water (a little at a time), mixing again.

GILDING

2 Using a third emulsion brush, dab the entire surface with glaze and then quickly rub off with rags so that the glaze remains only in the detailing.

3 Rub the gilding on the raised and highlighted areas with the other soft polishing cloth to buff up. Allow the remaining emulsion to dry (30 minutes).

Notes You can increase the ageing effect by gently taking back the gilding in places where the object would naturally become worn. Use a little wirewool dipped in methylated spirits before applying the sealant coat.

Gilding transforms a galvanized garden tub into something rich and strange: another variation on the basic recipe (see also p. 45). About 20 gold Dutch metal leaves were applied and sealed with amber shellac. The ageing glaze was coloured simply with 4tbsp coeruleum blue.

VARIATION – GOLD BROKEN LEAF

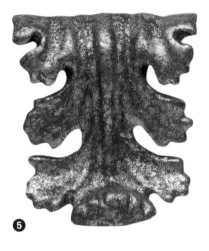

⑤ GOLD BROKEN LEAF
Follow the basic recipe for the base coat, sizing and gilding stages. You will need 100g (3¹/₂oz) broken leaf. Seal with a diluted amber french enamel varnish (170ml varnish to 80ml methylated spirits), using a 50mm (2in) household brush. Allow to dry (30 minutes). ⑤

As the name suggests, broken leaf is composed of the off-cuts and fragments created when making Dutch metal leaf. Gold and aluminium (see below) are available. You buy it by weight and it is cheaper than whole leaf. Broken leaf takes much longer to apply – to be honest, it takes some patience – but done well it creates a more worn, aged effect because more of the base coat shows through. There is no need to apply an ageing glaze.

VARIATION – COPPER LEAF

⑥ COPPER LEAF
As basic recipe for base coat, sizing and gilding, using 12 copper leaves. Seal with 250ml clear satin acrylic varnish, applied with a 50mm (2in) brush. Allow to dry (1 hour). Finish with a blue ageing coat (2tbsp white vinyl silk emulsion, ¹/₂tbsp neutral grey, scant 1tsp ultramarine blue and 2tbsp water).

Theatricality is really the keynote here, although copper Dutch metal leaf gives a less opulent effect than the more traditional gold leaf. I think it works well in contemporary interiors, and in particular with more unusual *objets d'art* and ethnic collections. If you have a taste for the less predictable, you could experiment with different coloured French enamel varnishes for the sealant coat (see sample 5 for the proportions). I have sometimes used bright red to create an exciting, modern effect.

⑥

VARIATION – ALUMINIUM LEAF

⑦ ALUMINIUM LEAF
The process and quantities are as for the basic recipe, but use a premixed blue vinyl matt emulsion for the base coat, seal with transparent acrylic scumble glaze instead of shellac, and omit the yellow ochre from the ageing ingredients.

⑦

Aluminium Dutch metal leaf is used to create a silver-leaf finish. Again, like copper leaf, it seems to suit modern interiors best. Premixed blue or green vinyl matt emulsion is substituted for red oxide primer (or deep red emulsion) at the base-coat stage because either will complement the silver well. In the sample shown here I used a mid-tone blue, but if you like bold, contemporary effects try experimenting with the darker tones of either colour.

STENCILLING

Stencilling is a good way to disguise uneven walls and is excellent combined with a paint-finished base. It works well on simple furniture too. Ready-made stencils are available from specialist shops and DIY chains, but you can easily design your own for a more individual look. Decoration and pattern books are available at libraries and you can also find inspiration in your own home – wallpapers, carpets and tiles, all spark off ideas. Begin with simple designs like those given here, and, when you have mastered the technique, be more adventurous.

BASIC RECIPE – BLOOMSBURY LEAF IN MINT AND BLUE

INGREDIENTS

Base coat ▶ 1 litre white vinyl matt emulsion / 1tbsp raw umber artists' acrylic colour / 1tbsp yellow ochre artists' acrylic colour
First stencil colour ▶ 250ml white vinyl matt emulsion / 2 tbsp bright aqua green artists' acrylic colour / 1tbsp bright green artists' acrylic colour
Second stencil colour ▶ 250ml white vinyl matt emulsion / 2tbsp cobalt blue artists' acrylic colour / $1/2$tbsp neutral grey artists' acrylic colour
Optional protective coats ▶ 700ml clear matt acrylic varnish (two coats)

EQUIPMENT

Photocopier (optional) / pencils (1 soft, 1 hard) / tracing paper / ruler / stencil card (oiled manilla or cardboard sealed with linseed oil) / fine black pen / cutting mat or strong card / craft knife / 3 containers for mixing paint / 1 x 50mm (2in) emulsion brush / masking tape / rag / 2 small jars for holding paint / 2 stencil brushes /1 x 50mm (2in) varnish brush (optional)

INSTRUCTIONS
Making the stencil

1 Photocopy the design from one of the samples shown opposite, enlarging it to the size you want. If you do not have access to a photocopier, copy the design to size freehand or trace it and then, drawing a grid of intersecting lines over the design to help you copy it accurately to scale, enlarge it.
2 Trace the correctly sized design onto tracing paper and lay the tracing face-down on a piece of stencil card large enough to allow a mask of 10cm (4in) around the design.
3 Rub a soft pencil over the reverse side of the traced lines to transfer them to the card.
4 Remove the tracing and, using a harder pencil, draw the lines in lightly. Then go over the lines again, this time using a fine black pen.
5 Protecting your work surface with a cutting mat or strong piece of card, cut out the stencil with a craft knife.
6 Trim the mask (see step 2), using the ruler and craft knife.

Base coat

1 Pour the emulsion into one of the containers. Add the raw umber and yellow ochre and stir well.
2 Apply evenly (see p. 34) to your prepared surface, using the emulsion brush, and allow to dry (2–3 hours).

PAINT RECIPES

The Bloomsbury leaf design was here rescaled for random and formal use on walls, furniture and a MDF magazine rack.

To create the border, I marked the edge of the mask once the first motif was in position and used that as a guide when positioning the second motif and so on.

This colourway uses the following tints. Base coat: 6tbsp cadmium yellow. First stencil colour: 2tbsp red oxide and 1tbsp cadmium red. Second stencil colour: 2tbsp cobalt blue and 1tbsp turquoise light.

First stencil colour

1 Position your stencil on the base coat, using light pencil marks to guide you if necessary. Secure it with small pieces of masking tape. It is best to remove most of the tackiness on a rag before using the tape so that you do not lift paint off the wall when you remove the stencil.

2 Pour the emulsion into a second container. Add the bright aqua green and bright green and stir well.

3 Decant a little paint into one of the small jars: it is much easier to work with small quantities. Dip just the tip of one of the stencil brushes into the paint – 5mm (^{1}/4in) is quite enough. It is important not to overload your brush because the paint may bleed underneath the stencil. Using a light, tapping movement, stipple the paint onto the base coat

❶ MINT AND BLUE The colourway of the basic recipe.

❷ PINK AND LILAC Here the base coat is coloured with 4tbsp light portrait pink. The first stencil colour is created by mixing 2tbsp light portrait pink and 1/2tbsp cadmium red, while the second is simply tinted with 2tbsp pale violet.

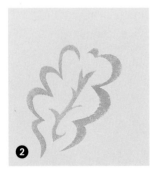

185

through the cut-out areas. You are aiming to paint one edge of the leaf and the central vein with this colour. Work slightly over the mask to make sure the whole area is covered.

Adding the first colour (see p. 185 top, for colourway).

Second stencil colour

1 Pour the emulsion into a third container. Add the cobalt blue and grey and stir well.
2 Decant a little paint into the other small jar. Using the same method, apply the second colour to the other edge of the leaf, again working over the mask a little. Remove the masking tape and lift the stencil carefully off the surface. Allow to dry (30 minutes).

Notes For a hardwearing finish in a hallway, kitchen or bathroom apply two coats of matt acrylic varnish just to the stencilling. Allow 2–3 hours for each coat to dry.

VARIATION – STENCILLING WITH DUTCH METAL LEAF

The simple technique of stencilling can easily be adapted to use gilding (see pp. 26 and 180). Once the stencil is positioned and secured with masking tape on your prepared and painted surface (see p. 184), brush a thin, even coat of Italian water-based size through the stencil, using a 12mm (1/2in) flat artists' brush. (Shake or stir the size before use, following the manufacturer's instructions, and do not overload the brush or you will make bubbles in the size.) Allow to dry until transparent (20–30 minutes) and remove stencil carefully.

❸ **SILVER-LEAF STENCIL** Stencilling with Dutch metal leaf. To create 25 crowns (10cm/4in high) I used 20 leaves and 200ml Italian water-based size. The crowns are sealed with 200ml acrylic varnish and left to dry for 30 minutes.

The base coat is sponged: add 2tbsp red oxide artists' acrylic colour and 1tbsp raw sienna artists' acrylic colour to 1 litre white vinyl matt emulsion.

❹ **COPPER-LEAF STENCIL** Copper leaf applied and sealed as sample 3. Here the base coat is blue, mixed as described opposite (above).

Put on protective gloves and, lifting up a leaf of gold Dutch metal leaf, lay it carefully on the sized area. Gently remove the excess leaf, using a soft-bristled burnishing brush: position a dustsheet or large box under the brush as you work to catch some of the fragments. Then polish the burnished leaf with a soft cloth and reposition the stencil carefully, once again securing with masking tape. Apply a thin coat of amber shellac to the leaf, using another flat artists' brush. Remove the stencil and allow to dry (30 minutes).

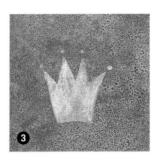

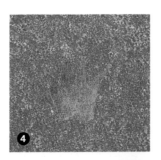

⑤ SPONGED AND GOLD-LEAF STENCIL
A simple square (20 x 20cm/8 x 8in) stencil was used for the chequered base coat. One colour was sponged onto alternate squares premarked on the wall and allowed to dry (2–3 hours) before the other colour was applied.

Blue: 2tbsp cobalt blue and 1tbsp neutral grey added to 500ml white vinyl matt emulsion. Soft ochre: 2tbsp yellow ochre and 1tbsp raw sienna added to 500ml white vinyl matt emulsion.

The gold Dutch metal leaf crowns were applied and sealed as sample 3.

RUBBER STAMPING

Much the same effect can be achieved more simply and more cheaply by using a rubber-stamp design and gold paint. Many specialist print shops will order rubber stamps to your specification, and a roller is usually supplied with the stamp or can be bought from an artists' supplies shop. Pour a little gold paint onto a saucer and roll the roller through it, making sure it is completely covered in paint. Then roll the paint over the stamp until it is covered. Place the stamp on your prepared and painted surface and rock it backwards and forwards: the stamp is slightly curved so this rocking action is essential for a complete impression of the design. Lift the stamp off carefully and allow to dry (30 minutes).

Gold paint is rolled onto the rubber stamp. Remember to rock the roller to make sure the surface is completely covered before you begin to work.

⑥ GOLD RUBBER STAMPING
Gold paint on an ochre base coat (see above): the resulting impression is sharper but less rich than the gold-leaf stencil.

⑦ BLUE RUBBER STAMPING
Blue paint mixed to the recipe given in sample 5 is used for this impression. The base coat is again soft ochre.

LIST OF SUPPLIERS

Most of the materials and equipment described in this book can be found either in your local artists' supplies shop or DIY warehouse. If you have difficulty finding any of the more specialized brushes and materials, consult the list below. A number of the companies listed here have mail-order facilities. However, bear in mind that some suppliers will not dispatch toxic or inflammable materials by post.

✉ Indicates that a mail-order service is available.

SPECIALISTS

Craig and Rose plc
172 Leith Walk
Edinburgh EH6 5EB
0131–554 1131
Traditional varnishes

The English Stamp Company ✉
Sunnydown
Worth Matravers
Dorset BHI9 3JP
01929 439117
Pre-made and made-to-order rubber stamps and paints

Liberon Waxes
Mountfield Industrial Estate
Learoyd Road
New Romney
Kent TN28 8XU
01797 367555
Gold waxes

Nutshell Natural Paints ✉
New Take
Staverton
Devon TQ9 6PE
01803 762329
Excellent range of powder pigments

Plasterworks
38 Cross Street
Islington
London N1 2BG
0171–226 5355
Architectural cornices and mouldings and plaster objects and details, plus restoration

Scumble Goosie ✉
1 Cotswold Place
Chalford Hill
Stroud
Gloucestershire GL6 8EJ
01453 886414
Unpainted and painted MDF and wooden interior accessories

Stuart Stevenson
68 Clerkenwell Road
London EC1M 5QA
0171-253 1693
Gold and silver leaf and related gilding products

GENERAL

Brodie and Middleton Ltd ✉
68 Drury Lane
London WC2B 5SP
0171–836 3289
Brushes, lacquer paint, metallic powders, oil and acrylic paints and powder pigments

Cornelissen and Son Ltd ✉
105 Great Russell Street
London WC1B 3RY
0171–636 1045
Gilding materials, powder pigments, oil and acrylic colours

Green and Stone ✉
259 King's Road
London SW3 5EL
0171–352 0837
Brushes, crackle varnishes, linseed oil, milk paints, oil and acrylic colours, scumble glazes, shellac, stencil card and equipment

John T. Keep & J.W. Bollom
15 Theobalds Road
London WC1X 8FN
0171–242 7578
Brushes, crackle varnishes, oil and acrylic colours, powder pigments, scumble glazes and universal stainers

John Myland Ltd ✉
80 Norwood High Street,
West Norwood
London SE27 9NW
0181–670 9161
Gesso, polish, sandpapers, varnishes and wood finishes

Omnihome Ltd
77 Goldbourne Road
London W10 5NP
0181–964 2100
Brushes, oil colours and varnishes

E. Ploton (Sundries) Ltd ✉
273 Archway Road
London N6 5AA
0181–348 2838
Bronze powders, brushes, gilding materials, oil and acrylic colours and powder pigments

Wood Finishes
30 The Vineyard
Richmond
Surrey TW10 6AN
0181–332 1772
Gilding materials, lacquer paint, powder pigments and spirit dyes

HISTORICAL PAINTS/COLOURS

Fired Earth plc ✉
Twyford Mill
Oxford Road
Adderbury
Oxfordshire OX17 3HP
01295 812088

Fired Earth plc
21 Battersea Square
London SW11 3JF
0171–924 2272

Fired Earth plc
102 Portland Road
London W11 4LX
0171–221 4825
Range of 'Pugin' colours, suitable for 19th-century interiors

National Trust Paint Range
c/o Farrow and Ball
(Southern) Ltd
Uddens Trading Estate
Wimborne
Dorset BH21 7NL
01202 876141

Paper and Paints
4 Park Walk
London SW10 0AD
0171–352 8626
Also colour matching and specialist paints and supplies

The Rose of Jericho Ltd
PO Box 53
Kettering
Northamptonshire NN14 3BN
Also traditional materials

BIBLIOGRAPHY

Bennell, Jennifer. *Master Strokes*, Century, London, 1988.

Drucker, Mindy and Pierre Finklestein. *Recipes for Surfaces*, Cassell, London, 1993.

D'andrea Cennini, Cennino. *The Craftsman's Handbook (Il Libro Dell' Arte)*, reprinted by Dover, New York, 1960. A guide to paint techniques written in 15th-century Florence.

Hilliard, Elizabeth. *The Library of Interior Detail / Cottage: English Country Style*, Pavilion, London, 1994.

Massey, Robert. *Formulas for Artists*, Batsford, London, 1968.

Sloan, Annie and Kate Gwynn. *The Complete Book of Decorative Paint Techniques: A Step-by-Step Source*, Ebury Press, London, 1992.

Stewart, Bill. *Signwork: A Craftsman's Manual*, Collins: BSP Professional, London, 1984.

Wainwright, Clive. *The Romantic Interior: British Collector at Home, 1750–1850*, Yale University Press, 1989.

INDEX

INDEX

ACKNOWLEDGMENTS

AUTHOR'S ACKNOWLEDGMENTS

Firstly I want to thank Mark for all the prop- and model-making, for the expert ageing techniques and for all his hard work. The book could not have been published without him. A big thank you to Lord and Lady Cobbold too; it was their encouragement and the inspiration of Knebworth House itself that helped me turn a corner in my life. Thanks too to Gabi Tubbs for having faith in me, to Quadrille, Patrick McLeavey and Jo Brewer for all their support, to Mary Davies and her amazing feats (I expect great things from her in the paint-effects department), and to Debbie Patterson and Linda Burgess for their beautiful location shots. Thanks also to Bob, Maurice and Sam and all at Courier Cars for the wonders they performed; John at Scumble Goosie for his lovely work and that magazine rack; and the crew at Plasterworks. Lastly, thanks to anyone I have not mentioned who played a part in the creation of this book.

PICTURE ACKNOWLEDGMENTS

The publisher wishes to thank the following photographers and organizations for their kind permission to reproduce the photographs in this book:

2 Pascal Chevallier/*Agencé Top*/Michel Klein's house, Provence; 4 David George/*Elizabeth Whiting & Associates*; 5 Debbie Patterson; 6 Simon McBride/*Country Living Magazine*; 7 Ianthe Ruthven (Charleston Farm House); 8 top Pascal Chevallier/*Agencé Top*/Michel Klein's house, Provence; 8 bottom Simon McBride; 9 Paul Ryan/*International Interiors*; 10 James Merrell/*Country Living Magazine*; 11 top James Mortimer (designer: Christophe Gollut)/*The Interior Archive*; 11 bottom Tim Street-Porter (designers: Brett Landenberger & Scott Waterman); 12-13 Debbie Patterson; 48–9 Trevor Richards/*Homes & Gardens /Robert Harding Syndication*; 50 top Hugh Johnson/*Country Living Magazine*; 50 bottom Tim Street-Porter/*Elizabeth Whiting & Associates*; 51 top Christopher Simon-Sykes (artist: Celia Lyttleton)/*The Interior Archive*; 51 bottom Simon Brown/*The Interior Archive*; 52 *Elizabeth Whiting & Associates*; 54 Debbie Patterson; 55 Mick Hales; 61 Tim Beddow/*Country Living Magazine*; 66–7 top Pascal Chevallier/*Agencé Top*/Michel Klein's house, Provence; 66 bottom Simon Brown/*The Interior Archive*; 67 top right David Phelps/Courtesy – *American HomeStyle Magazine* (designer: Michael Berman); 67 bottom Ingalill Snitt; 70 Christopher Simon-Sykes (artist: Celia Lyttleton)/*The Interior Archive*; 74 Simon Brown (designer: Christopher Gollut)/*The Interior Archive*; 79 Trevor Richards/*Abode*; 83 Ian Parry/*Abode*; 86 top left Ingalill Snitt; 86 top right James Mortimer/*The Interior Archive*; 86 bottom Christopher Simon-Sykes (artist: Celia Lyttleton)/*The Interior Archive*; 87 Pascal Chevallier/*Agencé Top*/Michel Klein's house, Provence; 90 Tim Beddow/*Country Living Magazine*; 92 Tim Street-Porter (designer: Michael Anderson); 95 Jan Baldwin/*Homes & Gardens /Robert Harding Syndication*; 99 Simon Brown/*The Interior Archive*; 100 Richard Bryant (Costa Careyes Villa, between Puerto Vallarta and Nanzamillo on the Mexican Pacific Ocean)/*Arcaid*; 102 top Simon Brown/*Country Homes & Interiors /Robert Harding Syndication*; 102 bottom Gilles de Chabaneix (stylist: Rozensztroch)/*Marie Claire Maison*; 103 top Mick Hales; 103 bottom Ianthe Ruthven; 104 Debbie Patterson; 114 Trevor Richards/*Homes & Gardens /Robert Harding Syndication*; 120–1 Debbie Patterson; 123 Simon Brown/*The Interior Archive*; 125 Simon Brown (François Gilles)/*The Interior Archive*; 126–7 top Simon McBride; 126 bottom Neil Lorimer/*Elizabeth Whiting & Associates*; 127 top right Ingalill Snitt; 127 bottom Simon McBride; 128 Debbie Patterson; 131 David George/*Elizabeth Whiting & Associates*; 133 David George/*Elizabeth Whiting & Associates*; 134 Paul Ryan (Shinbach)/*International Interiors*; 136 Debbie Patterson; 140 top David Parmiter (designer: Martin Bass); 140 bottom Christopher Drake/*Country Homes & Interiors /Robert Harding Syndication*; 141 top Richard Bryant (Charleston Farm House)/*Arcaid*; 141 bottom David George/*Elizabeth Whiting & Associates*; 144 Ken Kirkwood (Penhow Castle, Gwent)/*Arcaid*; 149–50 Debbie Patterson; 155 Debbie Patterson; 156 top F. Nüttgens/Brigitte/*Camera Press*; 156 bottom Di Lewis/*Elizabeth Whiting & Asscociates*; 157 top Fritz von der Schulenberg/*Country Homes & Interiors / Robert Harding Syndication*; 157 bottom Gian Carlo Gardin; 159 Debbie Patterson; 161 Paul Ryan/*International Interiors*; 163 Linda Burgess; 165 Debbie Patterson; 167 Debbie Patterson; 168 top Tim Street-Porter (decorator: Tom Beeton); 168 bottom Huntley Hedworth/*Country Living Magazine*; 169 top Spike Powell/*Country Living Magazine*; 169 bottom Simon Brown/*The Interior Archive*; 170 Christopher Drake/*Homes & Gardens/Robert Harding Syndication*; 172 Andreas von Einsiedel/*Elizabeth Whiting & Associates*; 175 Debbie Patterson; 179 Debbie Patterson; 182 Debbie Patterson; 185 top Simon Lee/*Country Living Magazine*; 186 top Simon Lee/*Country Living Magazine*.

Special photography of paint samples, materials and equipment by Patrick McLeavey. The ladder illustrations are by Clive Goodyer and the illustrations on page 39 are by Caroline Della Porta.